Distant Minarets

Carl Richardson
and
David Roberts

Pen Press

First published in Great Britain by Pen Press

All paper used in the printing of this book has been made from wood grown in managed, sustainable forests.

ISBN13: 978-1-78003-483-6

Printed and bound in the UK
Pen Press is an imprint of
Indepenpress Publishing Limited
25 Eastern Place
Brighton
BN2 1GJ

A catalogue record of this book is available from the British Library

Cover design by Claire Spinks

Cover image: Louis Comfort Tiffany (American, 1848-1933). *On the Way between Old and New Cairo, Citadel Mosque of Mohammed Ali, and Tombs of the Mamelukes*, 1872. Oil on canvas, 41 3/8 x 68 1/16 in. (105.1 x 172.9 cm). Brooklyn Museum, New York, Gift of George Foster Peabody, 06.329

The authors

Carl Richardson is a great nephew of Matthew Richardson, grandson of Matthew's younger brother Ernie. He lives and works in Cumbria, and is a writer in his spare time, having published a novel, short stories and some non-fiction work.

David Roberts was the husband of Matthew Richardson's niece Sheila (née Richardson). David began the project to publish the letters that Matthew Richardson wrote during the time of his service in the First World War. He assembled the letters, did extensive background research, and wrote some of the text in the introductory sections and the annexes in the book. He typed out a preliminary copy of the book, which became the basis of the final, published version. Unfortunately when David died in 2007 the project was still some way from completion. A couple of years later, Sheila asked Carl if he would take on the project to complete it, which he agreed to do. It is hoped that this book, *Distant Minarets*, will be a fitting tribute to David's memory, as well as to the memory of Matthew Richardson.

This book represents letters and experiences from a very different time. The language used reflects the standard vernacular of the day. Every generation has its own language – the words by which we are classed and defined – and one can often guess a person's age purely by their choice of words and expressions. Just as many words have entered the English language since these pages were written, so too have many since passed from general use. Terms considered stuffy, archaic and even offensive by modern standards, were widespread at that time.

However, the intention of this work is to represent the words of one soldier writing letters home from the trenches of World War One. As such, they are reproduced verbatim and unedited so as to not misrepresent them and for the purposes of authenticity. However, no offence or upset is intended by their inclusion.

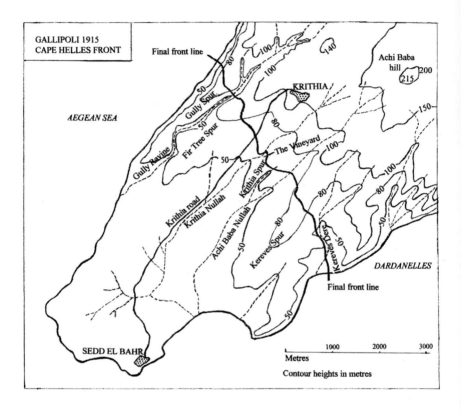

GALLIPOLI 1915
CAPE HELLES FRONT

Final front line

AEGEAN SEA

Gully Ravine

Gully Spur

Fir Tree Spur

Gully Ravine

Krithia road

Krithia Nullah

Achi Baba Nullah

Krithia Spur

Krithia Spur

KRITHIA

The Vineyard

Kereves Spur

Kereves Dere

Achi Baba hill

215 200

150

100

80

DARDANELLES

Final front line

SEDD EL BAHR

100 140
80 100

50

50

50

50

80 100

80 100

80

50

50

50

1000   2000   3000
Metres
Contour heights in metres

Index of letters and postcards

Matt taken in Khartoum 1914.

Introduction

For the great majority of soldiers involved in the wars and conflicts of recent times, letters from home ranked high in importance, as morale boosters and as a link with home in whatever far-flung place to which the war had taken them. Most soldiers also sent letters home, to advise their families of where they were and to let them know that they were alive and well at the time of writing. Many such letters have survived, preserved by later generations of the soldiers' families. What is unusual about the collection of letters published in this volume is that together they form a more or less continuous narrative of one soldier's experience of the First World War, from the time when he joined his local regiment in September 1914 to his final return to England, severely wounded, in September 1915. They also provide insights into one of the less well-known parts of the British Empire, the Sudan, at the time of its formal annexation to the Empire and into one of the other campaigns of the First World War - Gallipoli. Private Matthew Richardson wrote a good letter, inspired in part by the knowledge that he had appreciative readers back home who showed their commitment by keeping up their side of the correspondence.

Matthew Richardson was born on 21 December 1892 in Manchester, one of six children born to Matthew Ridley Richardson and his wife Maria. Both his parents had been part of the great migration that had made Manchester the centre of the industrial revolution by the late nineteenth century. The Richardsons and Ridleys had come to Manchester from the North East of England and Maria (Newton) had come from Liverpool. Matthew's early life was difficult. Matthew

Ridley Richardson proved to be a less than responsible father and Matthew and his sister Sarah were eventually brought up by their great aunt and great uncle (who had also migrated from the North-East) who lived in Hulme and later Stretford (in Manchester). Their great uncle, Nicholas Ridley, worked for the Refuge Assurance Company and it was presumably through his influence that Matt (and later his brother Ridley) secured positions as clerks in the company's vast and ornate head office building in Oxford Street, Manchester.

It was whilst Matt was working as a clerk in the legal department of Refuge Assurance that Europe was suddenly plunged into war at the beginning of August 1914. The immediate public response to the war was an extraordinary upsurge of patriotic fervour. In Britain, by the end of September, more than 750,000 men had enlisted in the army, a figure that had risen to a million by the end of the year despite the horrifically high casualty rates in the early battles on the Western Front. In the heady days of August, it seemed that just about every young man wanted to volunteer. One consequence of this was the formation of 'Pals' Battalions' - battalions that were made up of groups of men from the same factory, office, bank or sports club who had enlisted together. Nine battalions of the Manchester Regiment were 'Pals' Battalions'. However, although Matt was one of a group of young men from the Refuge Assurance Company who enlisted together on 1st September 1914, they were assigned to one of the Territorial battalions, the 1/7th Battalion of the Manchester Regiment. The 1/7th was mobilised* on 4th August 1914 along with other Territorial battalions of the Manchester Regiment. After a short period at a training camp at Hollingworth Lake, Littleborough near Manchester, the new recruits of the 1/5th 1/6th 1/7th and 1/8th Battalions were sent to Southampton as part of 42 Division. On 10 September they sailed for Egypt, arriving at Alexandria on 25 September. Some units disembarked there. Other units, including the 1/7th, were destined for Khartoum. This must have been a surprise to the new recruits. The war was in Belgium and northern France, which would have been where they were expecting to be sent. There was fighting in Africa, involving the then German colonies of Tanganyika, Cameroon, and South-West Africa, but all these places were a long way from Egypt or even Khartoum which was a long way from anywhere. The Ottoman Empire (Turkey) had not yet joined the war. The deployment to Egypt was presumably to provide extra protection for the Suez Canal in case of a surprise enemy attempt to seize this vital waterway and also to acclimatise the troops to tropical conditions. After several months of deployment to Egypt and Sudan, the 1/7th, together with other contingents of 42 Division, were despatched from Egypt to Gallipoli on 3 May 1915. In early June, the battalions of the Manchester Regiment, as part of 42 Division, took part in the Third Battle of Krithia. It was during this battle that Matthew Richardson fought the action that earned him the Distinguished Conduct Medal. The Manchesters, as part of 42 Division, were the only Allied contingent that fully achieved its objective in the battle plan, advancing in the centre of the front, capturing Turkish trenches and more than 200 prisoners and advancing well beyond the Turkish front line. The other Allied contingents were stopped by Turkish resistance and failed fully to reach their objectives which meant that the overall Allied battle plan of advancing the front line was not achieved. The troops of 42 Division had to be pulled back, despite their successful advance, as they would have been left in a dangerously exposed salient otherwise. Matthew Richardson was wounded during this action and was evacuated to Cairo. He recovered from his wound and by mid-July was back in Gallipoli. The 42nd Division was involved in the battle of Krithia Vineyard in early August 1915, intended partly as a diversion to cover the Allied landings at Suvla Bay a few miles along the north coast of the Gallipoli peninsula. It was during this battle that Matthew Richardson was seriously wounded in the left arm. He was evacuated to a hospital in Alexandria where his left arm was amputated. Not long afterwards, he was shipped back to England. Elements of 42 Division remained in Gallipoli until the final evacuation of Allied forces from the peninsula on 9 January 1916, it having belatedly been accepted by the Allied Command that the Gallipoli campaign had been a failure.

*[The 1/7th had existed prior to that date, but was effectively reformed with the new intake of volunteers in August 1914]

The Gallipoli Campaign

The Gallipoli campaign had its origin in a request by the Russian government to Britain in early January 1915 for a new initiative against Turkey to relieve the pressure on the Russian army in the Caucasus where the Turks were on the offensive. By the time the British got round to drawing up a plan of campaign, the Turkish forces in the Caucasus had been beaten by the Russians and pushed back. However, there was a wider strategic objective. If the Allies could establish and control a corridor between the Aegean Sea and the Black Sea, a major supply route to Russia could be established. The value of such a supply route could not be denied and this made the strategic objective very attractive. Whether, if it had been established, the corridor might have prevented the later collapse of Russia and the revolutions of 1917 is a debatable point. The main proponent of the scheme was Winston Churchill, then First Lord of the Admiralty, who proposed a naval attack on the Dardanelles to force a passage through to the Black Sea. The scheme was opposed by Lord Fisher, Admiral of the Fleet, who had explored the Dardanelles as a junior naval officer whilst serving on board HMS Agamemnon. Churchill prevailed, however, and on 18 March 1915 an Anglo-French fleet sailed into the Dardanelles in an attempt to force a passage. The attempt failed - three battleships were sunk by mines or shellfire, three more were badly damaged and the fleet had to turn back. Despite this, it was decided to proceed with the landing of ground forces on the Gallipoli peninsula. The landings were badly conceived from the start. They were at the southern tip of the peninsula, giving the troops the problem of fighting all the way up the peninsula against formidable and well-prepared Turkish defences before even reaching the mainland. A landing on the mainland north of the Gallipoli peninsula would at least have allowed the possibility of a war of movement with a realistic chance of reaching Constantinople. No attempt was made to take the southern shore of the Dardanelles. So even if the landings in Gallipoli had succeeded, with the southern shore of the Dardanelles still in Turkish hands, the waterway would still have been denied to Allied naval forces. As it was, the Allied troops faced a hopeless task on the narrow, barren peninsula against well-prepared Turkish defences. Despite repeated attempts involving great bravery among the troops concerned the Allied forces were unable to break out of the two beachheads they had established in the initial landings in April 1915, at Cape Helles on the tip of the peninsula and at Anzac Cove just north of the headland of Gaba Tepe. The troops were inadequate in numbers and lacked proper support and with no safe hinterland behind them they were constantly subject to Turkish shellfire wherever they were - as Matthew Richardson mentions in some of his letters. An additional landing at Suvla Bay in August 1915 also failed to break out of its beachhead. Even so, it was mainly the pressing need for troops elsewhere, especially on the Western Front, that decided the Allied Command to abandon a scheme which, had wiser heads prevailed, would never have been attempted in the first place. In the end, the most successful part of the Gallipoli campaign was its abandonment, during which the Allied forces were evacuated from the peninsula with minimal losses between 8th December 1915 and 9th January 1916. Allied casualties in the campaign were at least 50,000 killed or missing, more than 90,000 wounded and many more invalided due to disease. As a result of the failure of the Gallipoli campaign, Winston Churchill, one of the main promoters of the scheme, was forced to resign from the Cabinet.

Britain and Turkey in 1914

The First World War brought to an end a curious arrangement that had existed between Britain and Turkey with reference to Egypt and the Sudan since the late nineteenth century. Egypt and parts of the Sudan had been absorbed into the Ottoman Empire in the sixteenth century, and remained under direct Ottoman rule until the early nineteenth century. Following an invasion of Egypt in 1798 by the French, who were then expelled by the British, Mehmet Ali Pasha was sent to Egypt with an army from Albania (another Ottoman province) to restore order. However, having done so, Mehmet Ali Pasha then established himself as a de facto independent ruler of Egypt. The Ottoman Sultan, Selim III, was not in a position to regain control of Egypt, so rather than lose face, he acknowledged Mehmet as his Viceroy in Egypt. This was a constitutional fiction, but it meant that Egypt remained nominally part of the Ottoman Empire for a further century. Mehmet annexed most of the Sudan to Egypt in 1824 and it was still an Egyptian possession in 1914. Mehmet's grandson, Ismail, who became ruler of Egypt in 1863, got the country heavily into debt to European banks as a result of a grandiose programme of modernisation, which included the building of the Suez Canal in 1869. The British Government bought the canal in 1875, after which British influence became dominant in Egypt. In 1879 the British had Ismail dismissed and replaced by his son Tewfiq, who was more compliant to British demands. This provoked a revolt in the Egyptian army which was put down by a British military intervention that included the bombardment of Alexandria by British warships in 1882. It also provoked a revolt in the Sudan. The leader of the Sudanese revolt, who was known as the Mahdi, seized power in Sudan after the siege and capture of Khartoum in 1885 during which the Governor of Sudan, General Gordon, was killed. It was another 13 years before the British were able to regain control of the Sudan when Lord Kitchener defeated the Mahdi's successors at Omdurman in 1898.

On the outbreak of war in August 1914, the Ottoman Empire initially declared itself neutral. However, German influence in Constantinople was very strong and led to the Ottoman declaration of war against Russia and the Western Allies in November 1914. This led to the British finally ending the constitutional link between Egypt and the Ottoman Empire. Abbas II, who as ruler of Egypt had nominally been the Ottoman viceroy, was dismissed by the British who declared Egypt and the Sudan a British Protectorate, no longer part of the Ottoman Empire, on 18 December 1914. The British appointed Hussain Kamal as the first Sultan of the new Protectorate.

Matthew Richardson evidently witnessed one of the ceremonies that marked this change while he was stationed in Khartoum (see Letter 21). In view of his subsequent service in Gallipoli, it is strange to think that prior to the Turkish declaration of war, Matt and the 1/7th Manchesters, being in the service of the Khedive of Egypt (the title of the Egyptian ruler at that point) were therefore nominally in the service of the Ottoman Empire!

Note on the text

The text of the letters is reproduced verbatim, including spelling and grammatical errors, with editorial intervention [in square brackets] only where the meaning is unclear or where the handwriting is occasionally indecipherable. The opinions expressed are not untypical of the time, and readers should bear that in mind. The letters are historical documents. Some of the letters are written on stationery supplied by the Y.M.C.A. which, right from the start of the war, provided a range of welfare and support services in many of the theatres of war as well as in the UK. Most of the letters, however, are written on whatever bits of paper were available at the time. Many of them, including all those from Gallipoli, are written in pencil. The trenches were not conducive to the refinement of writing with pen and ink.

Photographs

All the photographs published in this book are from Matthew Richardson's photo collection. They include a number of photographs taken during the time when he was in the Sudan and Egypt, probably by his friend Ernie Shaw, who is mentioned in several of the letters. None of these photographs has any identification, so the suggested identification given in the picture captions may or may not be accurate.

Addressees

Auntie: Jane Ridley, Matt's great aunt on his father's side of the family. Her familiar name, which Matt often used in his letters, was Marny. She was Nicholas Ridley's sister (not his wife). She never married.

Uncle: Nicholas Ridley, Matt's great uncle. He was the brother of Jane. He never married. Nicholas and Jane spent most of their lives living at 91 Cromwell Road, Stretford, which was at the centre of family life for the Richardson and Ridley family for many years.

Cissie, Cis, Little Sister, Big Sister, Kid, Betty: Matt's elder sister Sarah Elizabeth who lived with Matt at the home of Jane and Nicholas Ridley in Stretford. 'Cissie' was her familiar name. Her fiancé (whom she later married) was Harold Adamson.

Mr Harrison (John): Matt's boss in the legal department of the Refuge Assurance Company. John Harrison's younger brother Edward (Ted) also volunteered and is mentioned in the letters.

Teddy, Ted: Matt's elder brother, who was also in the army, serving on the Western Front during the time when Matt was in the Sudan and Gallipoli.

Ridley, Rid: Ridley, one of Matt's younger brothers, who later also worked at the Refuge Assurance Company. Matt's two other younger brothers are also mentioned in the letters - Ernie, who was 20 in 1915, and Harold, who was still only a child. Harold is only mentioned once - bar this, references to 'Harold' in the letters are to Cissie's fiancé Harold Adamson.

Ma: Matt's mother, Maria Richardson (née Newton).

Tommy: pet cat.

Letters Home

Letter 1 - 5th September 1914

'H' Company, 7th Battalion, M/c Terr Regt.
Hollingworth Lake Camp
Littleborough

Dear Auntie,

I received Uncle's letter this morning and hope that there is nothing seriously wrong with him. He said that he didn't feel in form for anything but I hope that he'll soon buck up. I've been vaccinated and we have to be inoculated on board ship. This is perhaps the last chance I shall have of writing for some time. I've enjoyed it so far. I am on Town Picket tonight. I should think that the whole camp will be drunk as it is the last night in camp, we expect. We have to go round all the pubs and throw the Tommies out who are there. John Pieterson and the other chap have not arrived as yet. Perhaps they are keeping us waiting. I don't know but they cannot get equipment.

We were out skirmishing this morning. They aren't half putting we recruits through it, but I'm sticking it like a Briton. I hope that you won't worry at all about me and tell my Uncle not to as you will make me sorry I've joined if you don't take it like sports. Mr & Mrs Shaw have just been up to see us and Mrs Shaw is quite resigned to it by now. We received 5/- yesterday and were told that we would get another 10/- on board. Tell Betty that it will be her turn for a letter next. Hope that she won't be giving anybody the glad-eye when selling White Heather. I'm just writing about Ridley. Well I will conclude now so buck up. We rise at 5-0 am in the morning. Ugh!

I remain
Your loving nephew
Matt

Letter 2 - 7th September 1914

'H' Company, 7th Battalion M/c Terr Regt.
Hollingworth Lake Camp
Littleborough
Monday

Dear Kid,

We're here yet! We are all standing to, awaiting orders, but we think it will be Wed. There are various rumours abroad as to where we will be stationed, Cairo, Alexandria, Khartoom, Cyprus, Malta, Gibralter and various other places including Belgium, France and Germany. Well I'm feeling very fit and I don't care where we go as long as we see a bit of this little earth of ours. There are only two things I want - one is a razor and my football boots. Will you ask Uncle to rig both these up and send them. I think I'll get them all right. I got my Uncle's letter as I said before.

Harold and Maurice Shaw and Jenny came round yesterday. Pieterson and Newbould are both in our tent. Poor Jack, he doesn't seem to be made for a soldier. His girl, niece, nephew, landlady's daughter and his niece's boy, came on Sunday. They all seemed terrified. The grub has been splendid. In fact we beginning to suspect that we're being fed up for killing, perhaps for Christmas. We have two regular Sergeants drilling us this morning. Talk about language! Don't forget razor and boots will you. The razor I have here is like an old sword. Well, give my love to all at home and in Stretford generally.

Ta ta
Matt

Hope my Uncle is feeling better and my Auntie's eye is no longer gravy. You might send a rag for a dish cloth, too.

Letter 3 - 14th September 1914

on board S.S. 'Grandtully Castle'
Union Castle R.M.S.C
Tuesday Sept 14th 1914

Dear Uncle.

We arrived at Southampton on Thursday afternoon after travelling all night and the train went straight to the steamer's side. Consequently I couldn't get away to see Teddy or even drop a line as there were neither stamps nor paper available. We set sail at 6-0 on Thursday night and went out into the English Channel, where we waited until Friday night for the other Troopships. There are 14 Troopships and two warships acting as escort. The searchlights in the Channel were magnificent at night but when we got to the Bay of Biscay the joy was turned into sadness. Talk about rough. It was awful! Sick everywhere! It took us three days to get through and I should think that 29 out of 30 were sick. I wasn't, but I was feeling very queer. I am writing this on the deck rail so you can imagine that we are now out of it and we are past Cape Finisterre.

On board there are 2,600 troops and in the other troopships there must be another 20,000 and horses, guns and ammunition. We were all served with 100 rounds before leaving Littleboro' and I can tell you that the weight was quite sufficient for me. Our Company were on guard at the Station. It seems to drop in for all the guarding. Being H it is the last Company and is perhaps unlucky. I am on guard on one of the boats. When the alarm goes I have to double up with fixed bayonet and take charge of one of the boats. There are about enough boats for the Officers. That's all, but it's only red tape. We have had one alarm so far. False of course. Our destination is Khartum. We call at Gibralter, Cyprus, go through the Red Sea to Port Sudan and then by rail to Khartum.

The Major thinks that we will soon be moved from there to the lines of communication on the Continent. More medals! "It's a pleasure cruise," he says. I don't want to see the bay of Biscay again. We sleep on hammocks and they were swinging up to the ceiling. Quite exciting. We're packed like herrings below on the troop-deck, and what with the smell of people being sick, it's lively. We could look at nobody the last three days and food - we couldn't stand the smell of it even. Fellows were lying full length in the rain too bad to move. Thank goodness its all over now and we're in calm water.

The band is playing now and everybody is in the best of spirits. It's been very warm to-day and the sun seems to have revived everybody. By jove! It's made me appreciate the way Jane fed me at home. We're starting games on board but I shall not be able to take part as my arm has swollen up and is discharging a good deal. My shirt sticks in it and makes it worse. Ernie Shaw and I have been wishing we were at Khartoum and I shall be glad when the war is over and we come marching home in triumph.

I got Betty's letter just before we set out from Littleborough. Tell her that she ought to have been a local preacher. She tells the tale so well and makes it very interesting. Your letter didn't sound very cheerful. I hope you are feeling better. I hope the tennis court will be extended when I get back. How are the potatoes? And the chrysanthemums? On our boat there is the 7th M/c, the R.F.A. from Blackburn, Accrington Church, the A.S.C. and the Medicals.

I wrote to John Harrison about Ridley, and hope that he has heard something. I am absolutely broke! They don't pay Tommies in advance. I would only waste money though if I had any so it is just as well that I haven't any. Tommies are renowned for borrowing but I think they are much better at pinching. You have to watch your belongings every minute of the day. I got the razor and boots safely and I am much obliged. Credit my account with 5d. Has any money come from the Refuge yet? I hope you'll use it if you need any. It will be quite alright. Give my love to my Auntie and tell her not to start wearing my tennis trousers out after she has finished the shoes. She seems to think I have done a dirty trick in joining. I know you don't take it that way and I wish you would try and alter her opinion. I chuck it now and write more when we get nearer to Gibralter. Goodnight.

Wednesday Sept 16th 1914. What ho! Here I am again. We are nearing Gibralter but the boat has to go no faster than 6 knots on account of a French Ammunition Boat which has joined us and this boat is only a 6 knotter. She is bound for Marseilles but I'm pleased to say that she leaves us at Gib. There is a boat called for mails and we have to post them before 6 pm to-day. I was inoculated just before dinner. The doctor did it just below my vaccination which is very sore and I felt dizzy for about ½ an hour. It's gone off now however and I'm writing this basking in the sun. They have put awnings all over the boat and the heat is grand. It's much hotter than I have ever experienced in England but I can stand sun alright. At night all lights are out especially passing Lisbon. We passed Cape St Vincent this morning. The coast of Portugal looked fine in the sun. The stars at night look fine and in the day time the sky and sea are so blue and just a ripple on the sea.

I hope you'll be able to read all this scribble but there is not much accommodation for writing. Some of the Officers are wearing Pith Helmets and khaki drill suits and I expect they will be issued to us soon. How is the war going on?

I think that I would get a letter if you addressed it to:

Pte M R Richardson No 2263, 'H' Company,
7th Battn M/c Territorials   Egypt

It would perhaps be forwarded on to us. I think that Teddy was sent off before the 11th as we heard that a lot of soldiers had passed through on the Monday previous to the Thursday on which we left. On board they are a rough lot. Gambling and bousing all day long and the language! Of course our set is keeping away from it all except one or two who occasionally break out and either win or lose a few shillings. I'm not having any, however. Well, I've dried up now. There are no stamps on board and you'll perhaps have to pay 1d for this letter. Give my love to my Auntie, Betty, and all in Stretford and the surrounding districts, won't you?

> I remain
> Your affectionate nephew
> Matt

Unidentified photo from Matt's collection – possibly the
SS Grandtully Castle.

Letter 4 - 24th September 1914

S.S. 'Grandtully Castle'   No 2263 'H' Company
Union Castle R.M.S.C.   7th Battn Manchester Regt

Egypt

24th Sept. 1914

My dear Cissie (the one and only)

We're nearing Alexandria now which is at the mouth of the Nile. We are landing the R.F.A. & the A.S.C. there and are then proceeding through the Red Sea to Port Sudan where we train it to Khartum. If the heat continues I shall be reduced to a grease spot and a pair of braces. I'm Orderly for the voyage and have to work like a Trojan. (Is that spelt correctly?) Anyhow it's keeping me fit. The others are lolling about the deck all day and looking bleary-eyed. I got your letter all serene and was cheered up thereby. Pieterson has got a job in the Officers' Pantry and gets fed like a Lord. Chicken and goodness knows what. We, poor beggars, are having dry bread and tea for breakfast and tea. The Chief Steward and his satellites are cheating us out of our rations and mutiny is abroad. You can imagine the row that hungry men are likely to make. The language is fearful. Of course soldiers are always done brown on board a Troopship and it is an experience I shall not forget. If I get back, I'll never leave my Auntie again as long as I live. She can always have the priviledge of feeding me.

Last night and on Sunday Ernie Shaw and I were singing Chants and Anthems for all we were worth and shutting our eyes to it, thinking we were in the Choir. Poor Ernie Shaw, he feels the pinch of hunger very keenly and he looks at me occasionally with ravenous eyes. I suppose you got my letter from Gibraltar alright. We stayed at Gib. about 8 hours and got a fine view of the Forts and Straits and place generally. Are you having the Messiah this Christmas? I wish I was coming home for it but I don't expect we shall be home for a while now. We've been on board 2 weeks now and shall be on another 8 days approximately, and I don't think they would bring us all this way to send us back after a week or two. I hope to be back for Whit week. I hope you've extended the Tennis Court and put the wire-netting up.

I'm very short of paper and envelopes as this letter will prove. The paper acted as packing for my hat until this afternoon. My hat will drop over my eyes now and bury me. I have not much time for writing as my duties as Orderly keep me busy all day long. I have to feed wash up & clean up for 18 men so you can imagine what it's like. We have to swab the floor & keep things spotlessly clean to try to prevent disease which may easily break out with so many men on board. The boat can only take 700 comfortably and she is carrying 2000. We're like sardines. On board the Horse Boat 26 out of 50 horses are dead and the sharks are following us expecting further victims. Yesterday, we passed a Convoy of Indian troops, 22 Steamers full of them all sailing in line. It was a fine sight, I can tell you.

How is the war going on? We get no news on board and all kinds of rumours are in circulation. Some say it's over while others are very pessimistic about it. I do hope you'll be able to make this scrawl out as there is no accommodation for writing. Well remember me to my Aunt & Uncle and all at home and in Stretford and the surrounding provinces. I hope my Uncle is well and that my Auntie is cooling down as she generally does. I think she will be glad to see me when I come home. There won't half be a reception if we have our helmets on and drill khaki. The helmets look fine, I can tell you. We'll have some photos taken as soon as poss. Ernie Shaw is buying a camera out there. We have boxing and wrestling on board now and the boat is as steady as a rock. The Mediterranean cruise is very enjoyable when we stand on the top deck and try to make ourselves believe we've booked our passage but when we realise we're on a Trooper the novelty wears off.

Well, kid, I cannot get any more paper so I must conclude.

With best love
Your little brother
Matt

P.S. Help Tommy down the steps in my absence if she wants to go out and get into that gardening, you and my Uncle.

Matt's sister Sarah Elizabeth, or Cissie.

Letter 5 - 6th October 1914

'A' Double Company
7th M/c Regt.
British Barracks
Khartoum Sudan

6/10/1914

Dear Uncle

We have arrived in Khartoum and are now stationed in the finest barracks in the world. They are built on the bungalow system and the accommodation is marvellous. I might say that Khartoum is as near the Equator as any British Station in the Army and it is usual to send troops to milder places (to break them in) before sending them to Khartoum. We are the first Regt to be sent here direct. I will tell you more of the place after I have had a look round. I suppose you got my letter from Alex. and I will continue the journey from there.

Alexandria has an extensive harbour and found room for the 14 ships right away. The place itself is divided into the European and native settlements. The European part is like M/c except for the different dress and faces but the native part is composed of mud huts and the Arabs who live in them are the dirtiest in the world. You could smell them as they came on board to unload. The R.F.A & A.S.C. and two Companies of ours left us at Alex. and the other six Companys proceeded alone. We passed Malta in the night and landed at Port Said the following night. We stayed there all night and went up the Suez Canal early next morning. The canal is as wide as the Ship Canal at M/c and there is desert on each side. There are pretty military stations dotted along the route but there is nothing but sand and mountains to see as you go along. The Camel comes on the scene after Alex. and of course there are herds of them knocking about. We went through the Canal in 14 hours and were pulled up at Port Suez for the night. We had to have an Escort through the Red Sea on account of Foreign Warships being about and we waited off Port Suez for a Cruiser. There were five German prisioners in the harbour. One of the Nor Duetcher Lloyd* Liners going to Australia was one of them and she was a fine big boat. Well, we put off from Port Suez down the Red Sea and for a while could see mountains on either side. They looked grand as the sun set behind them and the moon was up in no time. There is no twilight here and you can see the sun sink. We made Port Sudan last Wednesday and were not sorry to get to the end of our voyage.

7/10/1914 We have relived the Suffolks who have been stationed here for the last 9 months. They came up to Port Sudan in two detachments and two of our Companies went back after the first load. We were the last to go and of course dropped in for cleaning up the ship. It takes 28 hours to get from Port Sudan to Khartoum by Rail, so we were at Port Sudan about 3 days. It is a grand place for bathing only it is not allowed on account of sharks. The water is as clear as crystal and full of fish of all sizes, shapes and colours. I went bathing about 5 times and no sharks collared me. I was diving into 30 fathoms of water from the jetty and you could see the bottom all covered with beautiful coral and sea weed. One day at Port Sudan the temperature reached 118 in the shade so you can imagine it is hot. You get a cool sea breeze at Port Sudan but at Khartoum the wind is hot from off the desert.

On the last of the Suffolks coming up we were fired off the boat and they embarked and put to sea straight away. We were left stranded, so we marched onto the desert beside the Railway and had tea, which consisted of dry bread and tea. We thought it bad enough on board but on a desert it tasted worse. However we got it down and had a game of football afterwards in the moonlight. After that we fell in and went to sleep, the Officers in front and the Sergeants in the rear. We were up at 4 next morning, and marched to the Railway in full pack at 9 o'clock and with our woollen clothing on and carrying rifle and kit bag, it didn't half knock us up. However the train was quite comfortable and we had 3 meals during the 28 hours of tea and bread.

We arrived at Khartoum in the middle of the day and had 2 miles march to the barracks in the blazing sun. One fellow from the Refuge fell over as soon as we reached barracks and is now in hospital with sunstroke. He is unconscious and was expected to die last night. We have to wear our helmets from sunrise to sunset and anyone found without one is put in clink. We are being issued with khaki drill tomorrow. We wear short knickers like boy scouts and shirts. That's all with putties on our bare legs. The Suffolks looked fine with brown faces, knees, chests and arms and I suppose we will look finer after a while. We have three blacks in our barrack room to clean up and do our washing etc. We pay them a piastre a week each man which is 2½ in English. We were paid 50 piastres yesterday which is 10/5. I get 10/5 per week and am putting in for a job as shorthand typist to the Adjutant which carried another 100 piastres a month or 5/2½ weekly. I may not get it on account of being a Recruit. The weather here is getting cooler every day and I understand will only reach 90 in the shade for the next 5 months. The rations are all very good here but things are very expensive and all tinned. Butter is 2/- a pound tin, jam 1/3 a pound tin and so on but you can buy a monkey off the niggers for 2 piastres or 5d. The Sudanese Band marched us to the barracks and they were trying to play cheery music. They march at a good pace and made us step out. The Sudanese are a very clever race of people. They all have three cuts on each cheek and the different angles at which the cuts are made denote the various tribes. The Native Army is very smart and the men are dressed in white smocks with a thick green sash and green in their turban and they can stand at attention until further notice without moving a muscle. I will tell you more about them later.

The barrack room holds 34 and we each have a bed, locker and rack. There are two electric fans going all day long and it is a very high room. We all have a folding bed, mattress, two sheets, blanket, pillow and pillow slip and we are kept busy cleaning rifles and equipment and straitening things up. Pieterson has been off sick for a fortnight. I think he is playing the old soldier a bit for he has had his equipment and baggage carried and now that we are all settled down he says he never felt better in his life. I am feeling in the pink. I'm as thin as a whippet but feeling strong. Ernie Shaw has had Diarrhoea for 7 days and is reduced to a shadow and as weak as a kitten. He is bucking up now I am glad to say and we are both falling out together closer than brothers. We both sleep on the veranda at night and the air is lovely and cool. We finish drill for the day at 7.30 and rise at 4, before the sun gets up. Even at 7 o'clock some of the chaps fall out, feeling faint. The mail goes to-night so I must hurry and finish.

I believe that the Turks are thinking of having a go. If they do Port Sudan will be one of the first places they will attack. They are examining our rifles here very often and it is a Dickens of a job keeping the sand off them. We are told that they are our dearest friends but I for one won't be sorry to say "Goodbye" to my dear friend as soon as the war is over, and we return home. We have been on the way nearly a month but I believe it only takes 15 days to get home. I am 4,500 miles away from Stretford but Ernie Shaw and I sometimes shut our eyes and fancy we are at home until our stomachs refuse to be kidded, and cry out for something to eat.

Well, I've about exhausted my travels so far so I'll chuck it. I don't know whether you'll be able to wade through all this lot as I've been interrupted many times and cannot get properly going. I hope you are all well at home. Give my love to Betty and my Auntie and all in the surrounding provinces and tell them that I'll never leave them any more. How is the war going on? We heard this morning that 75,000 Germans had surrendered but you cannot get reliable information here. Has Ridley heard anything yet and have you heard from Teddy? Hope you'll all write soon. It cheers one up to hear from home. I have to fall in now for our new clothes so I will finish now. Hoping that you are feeling well and pushing on with the gardening.

> I remain,
> Your affectionate nephew
> Matt of Khartoum
> Kitchener the 2nd

P.S. Kind regards to Tommy. We are playing the Garrison Artillery football tonight.

P.P.S. 'Cuse the smudges. It is caused through sweat off my arm and hand. You can perspire here as you lay on your bed. If you stop perspiring here, you might as well get ready for the next world. The water here is good and we are all advised to drink plenty to replace the sweat. The Suffolks sweat quite as much as we did on board the "Grandtully Castle." There are fine baths, hot & cold showers in the barracks and I believe we'll be allowed to bathe in the Nile. Beware the crocodiles!

*[Norddeutscher Lloyd]

*Unidentified photo from Matt's collection – possibly the
1/7th Battalion at Port Sudan or Khartoum.*

Letter 6 - 21st October 1914

'Cuse the blots and smudges
Which are caused thro'sweat.

My dear little sister

Your welcome letter (dater 28/9/14) arrived last Sunday and I thank you for it sincerely. I also received my Uncle's letter and was very pleased to hear that both he and my Auntie are feeling better. I was just getting downhearted when the Mail arrived and I got three letters. As I have said many times before, I am feeling as fit as a fiddle, and have done ever since the Bay of Biscay, when I got a few scabs scattered owing to the rough sea. Some fell overboard - liar! We are going at it pell-mell here. Went shooting early this morning. I did very well, I got two good groups - we had two goes each - 10 shots in all. After breakfast we had an hour's lecture on "The Attack" and then an hour in the Gymnasium, and then Bayonet fighting so you can see we've no time to sleep. The secret of health, here, is exercise whenever possible. I feel I could knock a house down.

Four of us went to Khartoum last Saturday and had a feed at the Hotel Gordon which is the best place in Khartoum. We had a fine blow out but, with a donkey back to barracks, it cost us 10 pst each or roughly 2/- each. I went to Church on Sunday like a good boy, and had a drink of limejuice in the aforementioned Café afterwards like a bad boy. The European women in Church are all dressed in light summer dresses of course, and the men all in white. A few had suits made of Shantung silk (Have I spelt it correctly?) We have all got our light drill and naturally look adorable. Ernie Shaw and I had our faces snatched this morning and will send them along next time - the photos not the faces.

Ernie has just gone to the hospital, sick. He does not feel or look very well, poor lad. We are bosom pals in this weary wilderness. We both sleep on the veranda at night side by side. We grow in beauty side by side. He has Diarrhoea and it's pulling him down. I tell him that if he goes much thinner, I'll be able to double him up and push him under their door when we reach Stretford. There are 8 cases of Dysentry and several cases of Malaria in Hospital and we had a lecture on these diseases last night. Malaria is contracted by a mosquito bite, Dysentry by drinking bad water. The water is put in big earthenware jars for drinking purposes and there is a tank underneath to catch the waste water and impurities. There is a tap on this tank and lots of us thought it was the proper thing to drink out of it. That accounts for the Dysentry or so they say. You have to use a dipper, which is kept in the jar. These jars, or Zears as they are called, are made of porous clay and have been used in Egypt for the past 4,000 years to my knowledge. The water is hot when it is put in but gets quite cool after a while. I drink about 2 quarts a day and about 1¾ quarts come through me, in the form of perspiration. There are good showers in the Barracks and I have a bath and shower every morning on rising. It is nice and cold before the sun gets out.

At Alexandria, a few of the Medical Corps came on board our boat off the "Avon" and they told us of all the good grub they got. The reason of it was because the Middlesex Yeomanry (I think it was) was on board and they comprised Solicitors and big-bugs of one kind or another. The 6th M/c left us at Alexandria and from all accounts they must be there or at Cairo. Some say they went on to India but I don't know how true it is. By jove! it sounds pathetic, the Defence Corps Voluntary Watchers. What are they watching? Other people's girls?

I'm glad my Uncle takes so cheery a view of the War. To-day we hear that Ireland has got Home Rule, Kitchener is in the field and that the Germans have put their last man in the field. We hear all kinds of rubbish here, the worst being that Turkey has declared war and were fighting for the Germans. That would seriously affect us in the Sudan, and everyone was preparing for a desperate struggle. Needless to say, the news was false.

I hope you'll be able to read this cramped up scrawl but paper is dear these hard times. I think you did right in not sending the Chocolate. The postage is too heavy and there is a scarcity of parcels with the English Mail when it arrives at Barracks. There are heaps of things which have been sent but which have not come to hand. I don't want any cigarettes as I haven't smoked since leaving England. Some fellows make you sick, going about with half-cigarettes in their ears and lighting up on every available opportunity. There's a Library in the Barracks and I read in my spare time, which is not often.

The chap with sunstroke is being sent home and they fear that he'll be an imbecile. I think I'd rather be dead than that. He was orderly with me on board ship and works at the Refuge. Of course it won't do to give his name, as he might get better. There are all kinds of reptiles round here - Lizards, Scorpions, Mosquitoes, Bats and numerous other weird-looking things. The sunsets here are quite African and look charming every night. The native men and boys look very well here but the women - the most ugly and repulsive creatures I've ever seen. Monkeys are handsome to them. Let me know all about Teddy won't you? I often wonder how he is getting on.

Poor Ernie seems to be in hot water. How about Ridley. I wrote John Harrison about it but perhaps they don't want two of a family in one department. However, I think he'll have no difficulty in getting a place when this War is over. I hope you'll buck my Auntie up a bit. I was pleased to get my Uncle's letter and will write him next time. It's no use writing two letters to the same place, is it. There's no reason why you cannot let my Mother read my letters instead of me writing over there. They're intended for you all, and I don't see that it matters to whom they are addressed. You're such a 'touchy' lot that I despair of ever pleasing you all. Don't forget to engage a Secretary and let me have plenty of letters, will you? I must now finish and hunt for stamps. We sometimes have to give fellows money to buy stamps and post our letters. Whether they buy the stamps or not, I don't know, but I hope they post the letters.

Well, I must chuck it now so with kind regards to Auntie, Uncle, Mother, Brothers, Sisters, Harold (and his relatives on both sides,) George and anybody else residing in the surrounding districts

I remain
your loving brother
Matt

Unidentified photo from Matt's collection –
possibly Port Sudan.

Letter 7 - 26th October 1914

No 2263, "A" Double Coy.
7th Batt'n Man. Reg't
British Barracks
Khartoum Sudan

26/10/1914

Dear Mr Harrison

We are now settled down to Barrack life and I have, at last, found time to write to you. The duties here are heavy and we are kept going practically all day long. The 1st Suffolks, whom we relieved, used to finish Parades for the day at 7.30 in the morning, but we have Parades at 6 o'clock, 10-30 and 4-30. In addition, we have Lectures and Gymnasium to fill in our spare time. The Barracks are said to be the best in the British Army and the accommodation is really splendid. Khartoum, I believe, is the nearest British Station to the Equator, so you may guess that it is fairly warm. We perspire all through the day-time and are naturally as thin as whippetts. Ted has lost stones. The water here is good and we are advised to drink as much as possible to replace the moisture lost by perspiration.

Our Batt'n is far from efficient and the extra parades are intended to smarten us up into Regular Soldiers. The extra duties seem to be playing havoc with the Troops however as two Sergeants have died since we came here. One died yesterday morning from Dysentry and he was buried at 4 o'clock in the afternoon. There are 8 cases of Dysentery in Hospital now, besides a large number of fellows with venereal diseases. The fellow from the Refuge, who caught sun-stroke, is being sent home next week with a number of others - with weak hearts, bad teeth weak eyes etc. Ted, Pieterson, Newbold and myself are all in the pink of condition. Personally, I never felt better in my life. I think I shall always winter in Egypt - hang the expense.

Port Sudan is a lovely place. We have one Company stationed there for 6 weeks at a stretch and I shall be glad when we go up there. We were there for 3 days before coming to Khartoum and it is ideal for bathing. The water is as clear as a crystal but there are sharks knocking about. I had 5 dips while we were there, without being disturbed. I understand that if you bathe in large numbers sharks won't molest you, unless they are particularly hungry. The water is teeming with fish of all colours and shapes. The River Nile is also full of fish but the water is fearfully muddy. I think it is called the Blue Nile at Khartoum but where the blue comes in, I fail to see. It ought to be re-christened the Brown Nile. There are heaps of crocodiles here and, in fact, all the creepy things under the sun, lizards, bats, mosquitoes and scorpions etc. In the town itself there is very little to see. The population is mostly Turkish with a sprinkling of Greek and English. I wouldn't stay in Khartoum longer than was necessary. It is so dreary, situated, as it is, in the middle of the desert with sand all round. The only place of amusement throughout the week is the Cathedral on Sunday. Really, it's not a place of amusement, but it's the only place where the British element can congregate. I have been to the service every Sunday night so far and it helps to remind you of home. Three fourths of the congregation are troops. The organ broke down last night and it sounded rather weird without the music.

Omdurman is only 5 miles from Khartoum and we intend visiting it next Sunday if we can get leave. We have to go in parties of not less than four. The Hill tribes in the surrounding districts are very fierce. The dum-dum bullets were first introduced in fighting against these people. I believe they're accusing the Germans of using these bullets but I think its far-fetched. We heard yesterday that Metz had been taken but we can never rely on the information we get here. There was great excitement last week. The rumour was abroad that Turkey had declared War on the Allies. Of course, the Sudan would be the first place which Turkey would attack and, as the Egyptian Army is chiefly Mohammedan, we expected being in the thick of the fighting very shortly. However it all passed over without the enemy attacking us at the Barrack Gates and all is quiet again.

Of course, I am in a Recruit Squad and we have Sergeant Instructors from the Regular Army instructing us. The language and sarcasm they use is very choice but it answers its purpose. The Instructor says that we'll lick the Trained Men into cocked hats in a week or two, and I can quite believe him, although I shouldn't say it myself. I am sorry to say that the Colonel of our Battalion is down with Malaria and I believe that he is being invalided home. He was awfully keen on the Battalion coming on Foreign Service and I dare say, he'll feel it very much. I hope I'm not boring you with this scrawl, but there's really nothing exciting to write about.

I had a gruelling last Friday, though. There were 10 of us told off as an armed Guard over some ammunition coming from the Station. The Station is 2½ miles from the Barracks and there were 100,000 rounds of ammunition to be carted to the Barracks. We marched there in the broiling sun armed to the teeth and proceeded to procure natives and carts to carry the ammunition. Well! All the old ramshackle carts and mules in Khartoum turned out and you never saw such an array in all your life. Loose wheels were tied up with rope and some looked as if cart, mule and driver would all collapse before they'd gone ten yards. I was on guard over two of these carts and first one would stop for repairs and then the other. I never worked so hard in all my life as I did over those 2½ miles back to the Barracks. The cartridge boxes were jumping all over the place and we had to push the carts through the loose sand. To make matters worse, one of the carts behind broke down and I had to drive one myself and look after two others whilst the driver was helping to put the wheel on the cart which had broken down. I don't know how we managed to get through with it all, but we delivered the 100,000 rounds alright, without splitting a box. Ammunition is packed in boxes of 500 rounds. I think a box weighs 80 lbs.

We're going on the range to-morrow to blaze some of it away. We were shooting on the Miniature Range last week and I tied with another chap for the best score. It is now 4 o'clock and as we parade at 4-30 I had better finish and get ready. I hope you are all keeping well at the Refuge. I dare say it's raining in torrents over there or else its foggy. Remember me to all in the Dep't.

Kind regards

Yours sincerely

Matt

P.S. I applied for a job as Shorthand-Typist to the Adjutant-General but was refused only on the ground that I was a Recruit and could not afford to spare the time. The job carried the magnificent salary of 25 piastres a week which is 5/= in English. I'm not sorry I missed the appointment. Enclosed is a snapshot we had taken the other morning.

Unidentified photo – possibly it relates to the 'ammunition convoy' (see Letter 7) – note ammunition boxes in the foreground.

Letter 8 - 27th October 1914

Khartoum

27th Oct 1914

Dear Uncle

Well, here I am again with my pen and ink. I got my Auntie's letter last Sunday and am highly honoured. I should think it is the first letter Jane has written for ages. I wish I had that milk-jug she talks about. I would drain it dry. Well, there's nothing very exciting here, but plenty of work. I had four Fatigues last week, one weighing fire-wood and three carrying ammunition. The best was last Friday. Ten of us were told off as an Armed Guard over some Ammunition coming from the Station - Khartoum Central. Well, we set off armed to the teeth and marched to the Station, a distance of 2½ miles, in the broiling sun. On getting there, we had to hire native carts to carry the stuff and all the old ramshackle mules and carts for miles round Khartoum turned out for the job. We picked 20 of the best out and they were crocks. Wheels tied on with ropes and goodness knows what. There were 100,000 rounds of ball cartridge to shift and, after much difficulty, we got loaded up. We had two carts each to look after and wheels were coming off here, mules leaving the cart in the shafts there and so on. One of the carts in charge of the fellow behind me collapsed so I took the other one whilst he and the two drivers attended to repairs. I had to drive one and guard two others. We all had to push through the loose sand and I can tell you I never worked so hard in my life. I can shout at mules and their drivers with anyone. We started out just after breakfast and landed back about 4 o'clock. The dinner was all cold but we were too tired to eat.

Another Sergeant died last Sunday morn from Dysentry and he was buried at 4 in the afternoon. There are 8 cases of it in Hospital now. I was playing football for our Batt'n against the Royal Garrison

Artillery, last Saturday afternoon, and we only lost 2-0. They are a fine set of blokes all over 5' 9" but we gave them a very good game. I was playing left back and it wasn't half hot. We had a look over the forts before the match and it is a very interesting sight. Talk about big guns. They are all mounted on swinging platforms and cover the desert for miles around.

There is likely to be some fun next week. The natives hold a Festival, equivalent to our Christmas, and usually get unruly. 50 of our men are being sent up to Sincat near Port Sudan where one of these meetings takes place and there is some scrapping every year. 68 of the Camel Corp are also being sent further up country. They are all armed with dum-dum bullets. These bullets were first introduced in fighting the tribes round about Khartoum. At Omdurman the natives were coming right up to the trenches with 5 and 6 bullets in them. It was in 1891, I think. You'll remember. They are picking out the old sweats for this job, and I'm not sorry. Oh! by the way! before I forget let me tell you that we had bacon for breakfast this morning. It's the first I've tasted for 8 weeks. I'll bet you'd miss the bacon if you were here. The excitement was so intense that I smashed my tooth - the one which had been crowned. It had worked loose and I bit a piece of hard crust and was lucky not to swallow the tooth. The crust on the bread here gets as hard as iron with the sun but it keeps your teeth sharp. Occasionally in the morning we get 'Herrings in Tomato Sauce'. It's tinned, of course, but we give it no quarter. The general fare is bread and jam.

We have started Musketry. We went on the Miniature Range three mornings last week and I tied with another chap for top score. I'm a knut at shooting. We go on the proper Range next week and blaze away some of the ammunition which I helped to bring from the Station. The Rifles are Lee Enfield Charger Loader marked '1 Star'.

Wednesday 28/10/14

Inspection is just over and in the half hour before the fall in at 10-30 I am going to do a bit more scribbling. Last night after tea we had a lecture on "General Gordon" by one of the Officers and a Concert.

There is a proper platform with foot-lights and we all had a fine sing-song. The Band was there, of course, and was the best turn of the evening. We had bayonet fighting and Gym yesterday. I went to the Cathedral again last Sunday. I was asked to play football again for our Batt'n but refused. I don't mind playing tennis but object to playing football in public on Sunday. I am sending a note for my Auntie. It is not an ultimatum but only a reply to her letter. I am also sending a snapshot which one of the blokes took the other morning. Our faces are not distinct as it was taken under a tree.

Ernie Shaw and I spend our evenings in bed instead of going out. We are allowed out till 10 o'clock but we don't get tea until 6 o'clock. After tea Ernie and I are usually tired out so we get our beds out on the veranda and are fast asleep by 8 o'clock. Neither of us have slept under cover since we left Alexandria. The night before last we got to sleep early and I was wakened up by the bugle sounding the 'Lights Out'. I could have sworn it was "Reveille" and didn't find out my mistake for a long time. I woke Ernie up and was getting my towel to go for a bath. It is quite dark when we rise in the morning but the sun soon comes out.

I'm sorry to hear that Ridley hasn't heard from the Ref. I'm writing John Harrison this mail but I won't mention it. It's a rule not to have more than one of a family in the place and I evidently haven't enough influence as yet to make them forgo the rule. I think he'll have no difficulty in getting placed after this War is over. Well, I'm about at the end of my tether now so will chuck it. I hope you are feeling better. Glad to hear my Auntie has got over the "Bronchitis." That's my complaint, isn't it? Don't forget to write as often as you can, oftener if possible.

Let's have some news about the War. We hear that Metz has been taken by the Allies but I cannot vouch for its accuracy. It seems too good to be true. I am still in the best of health. I think I will always winter in Egypt. It is getting cooler every day but is still unbearable in the middle of the day. I will have to fall in, in five minutes now so will close. With love to Betty and all at home including Jane, whom I am writing direct. There is nothing I want so don't waste money on postage. Au Revoir!

I remain
Your affectionate nephew
Matt

Nicholas Ridley - great uncle Nicholas. One might not have guessed from this rather fearsome portrait that in his spare time he was a skilled violin maker.

Letter 9 - 1st November 1914

Sunday 1/11/1914

My dear Cissie

The English Mail came in last Thursday and I got your letter dated 6th Oct. and also my Auntie's letter and the lemonade powder and newspaper. They all came last Thursday night, which was Christmas Eve out here. Last Friday was Mohammed's birthday or the Mohammedan X'mas Day and we had a holiday all weekend in consequence. The X'mas Festivities last for 4 days and during that time cannons are going off continually. It starts by 21 guns going off in quick succession and the noise was deafening. Some of the blokes in Town got quite alarmed and came running back to Barracks in great haste thinking that hostilities had commenced between us and the Egyptian hosts. The cannons are fired by the Sudanese Artillery from over the River.

Ernie and I were just thinking what a miserable X'mas Eve it was when the "Letter" Call sounded. "Cookhouse" is supposed to be the best call in the Army but I think "Letters" beats it, on Foreign Service especially. Our letters didn't arrive in the Mess until we were in bed but Ernie and I jumped out of bed and devoured our letters in our shirts. I consider myself very fortunate in getting something by each Mail. Some of the poor beggars here get nothing. You should see their faces drop when they are told that there is nothing for them. It's rotten, is it not? It makes me feel quite selfish, doing so well in the way of letters. It would have been a rotten X'mas Eve indeed, had the post not arrived, I can tell you. Ernie and I had 3¾d total between us and we were wandering about the Barrack Square wondering how best to expend it in order to celebrate the occasion. Ernie had a mineral water but I was more economical. I had a go on the Rings in the Gym, a drink of water and then went to bed. It was a lovely night and we could not help thinking of X'mas Eves at home. The nights here are all the same - clear sky, bright moon and large bright stars.

On X'mas Day, I was playing 'footy' again for our Batt'n. against the R.G.A and, of course, we lost. The only team which has ever beaten the Artilley is a native team of the Sudanese Army. They can play in the broiling sun until further orders, without feeling the heat. I don't know how you would go on here, kid, if you puff and blow at the heat in England. The other day a fellow's Dugaree caught fire. By the way you won't know what a Dugaree is. I'll tell you. It's about 12 yards of muslin, which is wrapped round your hat at the part where it fits on your head. It is supposed to protect your brain from the sun and stop softening of the brain. The bloke was on Police Duty in the middle of the day when it caught fire. So you see it is just a trifle too hot for spats. It is every day getting cooler and in December they say it will be too cold at nights to sleep out in the open. Ernie and I will borrow another blanket each for then. I will chuck it now and get ready for Church.

The Sirdar's Palace
Khartoum
On guard Mon: 2-11-14

Dear Kid

I am on duty at the Palace, Khartoum. We are guarding the Sirdar and his Staff and household. Palace Guard is the swankiest of Guards and its an honour to get picked for it. Well, I 'got the stick' again this morning, the meaning of which there is no reason for me to explain again. Of course we were all as clean as new-made pins and the Adjutant had considerable difficulty in picking out the best. I suppose my moustache did the trick. I've only had two Guards since being here and have got the stick on each occasion. Verily it is a noble record. I'll bet I'd get on in the Army if I was fool enough to sign my life away for King Jud. There's no flies on me, though. I want a bit of freedom, and the sooner this bally war is over the quicker. We were paid again last Saturday and Ernie and I had our usual flutter at the Hotel Gordon in true military style. We also made a tour of the provision stores. They don't mind you sampling the goods at these places and believe me, Ernie and I took full advantage of the privilege. We consumed more in "tasting" than we paid for in hard 'piastres'. We call a "piastre" a "disaster". Perhaps this will give you an idea how the word is pronounced. We intend going up to Omdurman on Sunday next. 8 of us are getting leave to go and we are going to buy relics. I am looking out for some Ostrich Feathers for you and Jane. I suppose you will wear them out and Jane will revive them and make herself nine hats of them. However, I've not sent them home yet, have I? I believe they are well worth sending home and you can rely on them being real Ostrich plumes. They are in short lengths, I understand. However, wait and see! I believe I could spend a fortune here on curios. That is the reason why I don't want any money sending. I'd only 'blue' it in rashly. I have 160 piastres in the Bank here. It sounds a large amount, don't it, but its only £1:13:4. It is the money which accumulated on board and at Littleborough. We get 6d a day extra pay here in Egypt. It is called the Khedive shilling. We would be much better off at home without it. At first, we were told it was worth 9d, then 8d but we only get 6d. Such is the way promises develop in the Army. With deductions for one thing and another, your pay looks very sick after it has gone through the various channels of stoppages. It costs us 10d a week each for washing. Of course, we would get our money's worth if we could have the things to wash, but when you've only two shirts and he calls one week for the dirty washing and brings it back clean next week, you cannot very well overdo the thing. We are, however, allowed to have two pairs of drawers or pyjamas washed per week, but as none of us posses the articles in question, it's a good thing slipping through our fingers. Never mind though, what you've not got, you can always do without. We are going to be issued with two new shirts each shortly. They have sent word home for a supply and, everything being equal, we should get them in 6 weeks time. There is no need for you to send anything. The postage is too heavy for one thing and it is bad form to have private wearing-apparel in the Army. If you are all short of stuff, you'll stand a good chance of getting an issue but if some possess things, they'll naturally think that the others have lost theirs or sold them. You see, I'm getting into a regular old soldier, while I'm stationed here. We've plenty of old soldiers in our Mess to instruct us in the art of getting as much as possible out of a 'generous' Government. On referring to Jane's letter, I see that she wants to know if I drink or gamble. No, I don't do either. I've not signed the pledge nor do I intend to. I've seen enough of the folly of both these things to keep me from it without signing bits of paper. Beer is 2 p.t. a pint here, which is 5d. You can get 4 bottles of mineral water for 5d, but I prefer water. You would be surprised how cold the water gets after it has been in the Zear for an hour or so. When you draw it from the tap it is hot! Hot enough to wash greasy dishes clean. Thanks for the Prussic Acid, it's quite a Godsend. I have just received your letter dated 12/10/14 and one from Edward. I am writing Teddie and shall be glad if you will forward it to him wherever he may be. It's hard lines having to stay at home twirling his thumbs, isn't it. It's sad about the poor Belgians. Fancy Jane getting "nutty" with Miss Hunt and the aristocrats from across the way. She is fairly cutting the Sands out anyway. Your cutting remarks about the sofa no longer sting. I wish I was on it now instead of in this Guard Room. I hope you'll continue to see to Tommy going down the steps at the double. I'll make the beggar "Slope Arms" when I get back. They are in a mortal funk here of the natives rising. I think the big guns have had an effect on their nerves. It's a fearful waste of powder and ammunition. I'll stow it now. Give my love to Auntie and Uncle and your Harold, won't you? It's about time my Uncle started wielding the pen. Jane is doing him in the eye fairly. Well, good-bye, kid, till next time. Don't forget to keep me posted up. I will now write to Ted.

With best love
Your loving brother
Matt.

P.S. You may, of course, have a look at Teddy's letter. I'm sick of telling the tale of woe about coming out.

Letter 10 - 10th November 1914

Khartoum, Sudan

10-11-1914

My Dear Uncle,

I got two letters by Sunday's Mail, one from Cissie and one from Jane but none from you. You're a slacker, letting Jane do you in the eye like that, but perhaps you haven't the gift of the gab like Betty and my Auntie. However, I've a lot of material this week so I'll get to business right away, without giving any further cheek.

Things are a bit brisk here with the Anglo-Turkish affair. Whatever it is, I don't know but we are fortifying ourselves round the Barracks for all we are worth, in the hope of seeing a bit of fun. We have double guards at nights, but sand-bagging is the worst job. Our Recruit Squad started firing on the big Range last Monday and I did fine. At the Miniature last week the Sergeant showed my target to the Colonel and he said it was very good indeed. It was a grouping practice. I got ten shots in about a three inch ring. Well, last Monday morning we went on the big range and I got a possible straight away. 5 bulls out of 5 shots at 200 yards. Not bad, eh, for the first time, is it. The Officer is telling everybody and has made me Commander of the Squad. He said, "Now Richardson, you've got the best score, march these men off the Range." I took them on the Range again last night and again this morning. To-day we started the Qualification Practice. You have to get 45 out of 100 for a pass, 68 for a 1st Class shot. This morning, I scored 15 at grouping and 18 at the bull out of 20, which was the top score again. I have got 33 so far and we have had three more shoots, so I stand a very good chance of passing out as a 1st Class shot. It carries an extra 6d a day in the Regulars, but goodness knows if we'll get anything in the Terriers. Last night at 200 yards the Major, four Officers and the Musketry Officer had five rounds a piece and none of them got a bull. It will, perhaps, make them appreciate what shooting is like. The Col. came down this morning and made 3 bulls and 2 inners - the same score as I got. It is a 7 inch bull at 200. We are going to the 500 yds to-night and rapid firing at a moveable target. At 500 the bull is a foot across, so I ought to get a few there. One chap in the squad scored 2 out of a possible 20 this morning, but the others are all tidy shots. Ernie Shaw got 10. He is not up to much. Did you hear that tale about the Sergeant Instructor taking an awkward squad on the Range? He took them to 500 and they blazed away without hitting the target, then to 200 but with the same result. Next he took them to 50 yards and still none of them could hit the target. Then he shouted, "Squad 'shun. Fix Bayonets. Charge! It's your only chance." And away they went and ripped the target to shreds.

We are raising a proper Regimental Football Team and last Thursday there was a Trial Match to pick a team to play against Khartoum City. I was picked for the Trial and the 22 of us got off parade, together with six Sergeants who were to judge the play. I was chosen to play for the Batt'n. and accordingly we were dished out with jerseys etc. The match against Khartoum City was on a Friday and there was a Parade at 4.15. However, the Colonel cancelled the Parade in order that the chaps could all come down and watch us. The ground is a grass pitch and there were goalposts, and nets and stands galore. The Team belongs to the Officers of the Egyptian Army and all the 'knuts' of Khartoum play for it. It is composed chiefly of English Officers and Instructors of the Egyptian Army. We expected a bashing but we managed to make a draw of it -2-2. All our Officers were there and, of course, the blokes. They made quite a fuss of us at half-time. Soda water, lemonade and limes in rare abundance. I don't care how soon we have the next match, although it is fearfully hot. The excitement was intense. I was playing wing-half and I had an Officer to mark. I never let him have a look-in, though.

I got a Guard for Saturday on the Powder Magazine. It is a rotten Guard and I tried hard for the stick. I was doing fine, until the Adjutant came to the "Examine Arms." He took a sudden dislike to my barrel, altho' I cleaned it well with the pull-through before coming on Parade. To show you what a lot they know about rifles, I'll tell you what happened the other day. It was Rifle Inspection and the Major was examining the rifles separately. He looked at one in the front rank and said "That's a very nice rifle. Always keep it as clean as that and you'll do." A bloke in the rear had a dirty rifle and exchanged with this man in the front. The Major looked at it and said, "When did you clean this rifle last? It wants a thorough cleaning out. Parade with it at 2 o'clock." He had said what a clean rifle it was only a minute before. The inside of my barrel is rather dull, I'll admit, but it shoots alright.

The Powder Magazine is about half a mile into the desert and is very quiet and lonely. The heat during the day is rotten for walking up and down on Guard but during the night, the two hours seem like 2 weeks. We have 2 on and 4 off. Round the Magazine is a high railing and the guard has to lock himself in from the inside and walk round. It is rotten not getting a night's sleep but it cannot be helped. We have two Guards each a week.

On Sunday last we got the day off and we went to Omdurman. There was eight of us and the natives gathered round us like flies when we got there. All the houses are built of mud and the natives are a lower lot than those in Khartoum. We bought all kinds of things between us and had a tribe of men, women and kids following us about all day. Jack Pieterson nearly got us lynched. He was buying a pair of slippers for 8 Piastres. He gave the chap 10 p.t. and by mistake the black gave him 2 5-piastre pieces change instead of 1-piastre pieces. Jack didn't notice it and so when the native found out his mistake he came after us with a tribe and was gabbering away like a grammophone. We were of course rather slow to understand what he was driving at. However, I told Jack to turn his pockets out and when the fellow spotted the 2 5 p.t. pieces we understood. He also caused a bit of trouble unconsciously an hour or two afterwards. He must be unlucky. A kid came with an earthenware jug to sell. When Jack got hold of it the handle came off, so he gave it the kid back and told him he'd clout his head, in English. However, the kid, not to be done, brought his father and all his relations on both sides and told them that Jack had broken the jug. The jug was worth 2½ p.t. with the handle on but the kid had pinched it from somewhere, and was trying it on. I gave him ½ p.t. for the jug and he went away grinning all over his face and thinking how well he'd done it on us.

There are no whites in Omdurman and the people are awfully poor and live like pigs. It makes you glad you were born in a civilised country to see the way they live. We were the only chaps to chance going on Sunday. The news of the war with Turkey came on Saturday. There are 500 British Troops in Khartoum and the nearest place for help if we should ever need it, is Cairo, 1200 miles away.

I got Cissie's letter and the Keatings and also my Auntie's letter. Also the P.O. for 3/6 which will be of much use when I get it cashed. I am broke with going to Omdurman and will send the bits of curios which I bought in due course. It's a nuisance sending things home. There is nothing to pack them up in. I will visit Omdurman again just before we come away and will bring home something in my kit-bag. It's a job to send things like spear-heads through the post. It's an art in itself buying anything off the natives. You must offer them half what they ask and get your money in your hand. They will refuse it of course so you must walk away and they will come running after you saying they will take your price. In Omdurman, they don't understand English at all and you have to make signs. I think they respect the British Troops, or we would have been chopped up. I have no need for the Keatings at present but will take a dose if I feel seedy, at all. I'm still feeling in the pink and Ernie Shaw is bucking up a good deal. We got a good deal of bayonet fighting and is it rare fun. We are padded and with helmets on we just look like divers. Tell Cissie not to bother buying me anything for my birthday. She must be on the rocks with Teddy and I. Tell her she shall have a new frock, from Khartoum. Let me hear about Ted, won't you?

Glad to hear that Harold has started doing 'Bobbying' as a profession. We could do with him on the Piano in the Canteen. Some fellows get on it and nearly drive you dotty, especially when you're writing letters. He'd have been in his element getting up Concerts here. We have one to-night, and a Lecture by an Officer who got his VC at Omdurman. Well, I must close now and get ready for going on the Range again at 3-45. Give my love to Jane, Cissie, Harold and all at home and don't forget to write and let me know that we're going strong on the Continent. Hoping you are in the best of health.

I remain
Your loving nephew
Matt.

Enclosed is another snapshot. Will get some proper ones taken.

Official portrait taken in Khartoum 1914.

Letter 11 - November 1914
Letter from Matt's boss at the Refuge Assurance Company

[Draft of letter from John Harrison in reply to Matt's letter of 26 Oct 1914]

Dear Matthew,

I was very pleased indeed to receive your letter of the 26th ult. and to gather as much from the tone of it as from the contents that you are in pretty fair spirits. What a tremendous change you must find it from the office daily round. I am thinking you will have a difficulty when the time comes to settle down.

There is little news to send and what there is you will have heard from Albert Shaw and others.

We have just had a rotten week of cold bleak winds and driving rain. The fellows in England under canvas (I understand there are still some) must have had a bad time.

Perhaps since your letter was written, things will have livened up a bit in Khartoum. I see that a lot of Colonial Troops have arrived in Egypt to help you against the Turks.

Your description of the transport of the Ammunition from the Station to the Barracks was entertaining, but one would have thought there would have been proper wagons provided for the purpose in an up to date place like the Military Barracks at Khartoum.

Manchester has just completed its 8th City Batallion of "Pals". The last Bat. was "Bobs Own" of men between 5 and 5/3. Most of the Civilians left in England are joining local Vol. Defence Corps. It remains to be seen whether we shall ever be of any practical service, even if necessity should arise. The War Office are giving some semi-recognition to the Corps under certain conditions. But what efficiency can be expected of a body of men which drills at the outside 2 hours per week. There's a bit of a difference between that and 5 or 6 hours per day.

I hope this will reach you by Christmas and I close wishing you all, Ted, Pieterson, Newbold and yourself a merry Christmas and a grand 1915.

Yours sincerely
J.H.

Letter 12 - 7th December 1914

Khartoum Dec 7th 1914

My dear Cissie,

Last night I received your letter and my Auntie's. I also got the map of Europe and have wiped my nose on Germany with rare gusto. I notice that Harold addressed the envelope containing your letter and the "handky" and hope that it may be a step towards dropping me a line or so. I received a missive from George Titterington but may not have time to reply this time.

This week our Coy. has all the duty men to find whilst the other Coys have a week's good training. We had a full week last week. Ernie Shaw and I are on Police Duty all this week. Two hours on and two off. It's a dreary job after dark. The Guards we have to find are as follows:- Palace Guard, Powder Magazine Guard, Diffusible Mag. Guard, Officers Quarters Guard, Hospital Gate, Donkey Gate, Camel Guard, quarter Guard, and Guards (or Police) for three entrances into the Barracks - Officers, Sergeants and others. So you see that we will have plenty to do this week. It is one night in bed and a night on guard. From the latest news on going to press we leave here on 18th Feby for Marseilles. I think we are bound to go before the Pals. Regt as we are in fine fettle and from all accounts the Pals. don't seem to be very well officered. We are badly off in that direction, but our Batt'n possesses some smart men and the other Officers are getting into ship-shape with all speed. Fancy Doug Sproat being at the Front so soon. He's a brick. It is awful hard lines on Teddy's two pals and I hope Ted will pull through without a scratch.. Their Regt got a terrible gruelling.

Last week we started firing our Trained Soldiers Course of Musketry. It's a very stiff test and if we pass out as 1st Class Shots we'll get an extra 6d a day. Among the tests we have to fire 15 rounds at 500 yards in a minute, with bayonet fixed. So far, I'm 8th on the list out of our Platoon. Our Platoon is going up first. There are 50 in each Platoon and 16 Platoons in a Batt'n. We are in the same formation as the Regular Army. The Batt'n is divided into 4 Coys. and each Coy. into 4 Platoons. Last week we were practicing the "March Past." The Sirdar intends to inspect the Batt'n soon and it may rest with him whether we get a move or not.

There's a fellow from our Coy. been writing all sorts of rubbish to his Ma to buck her up and it seems she has had the letters published. He not half been going through the mill. It sounded an awfully silly letter. Such phrases as "You should see us in our helmets. We don't half look a treat etc. etc." "Having a gentleman's life, finished at 7.30 for the day." He is a lad of about 17 years of age and is not responsible for what he writes.

My Auntie's letter is not very encouraging and I hope she won't write when she feels in the dumps. She must buck up and write a bit more cheerful. It's ridiculous getting excited over a Cake. As I've said before, I would rather not have anything sent than that you should squabble about it. I don't mind as long as I get plenty of letters. I sent you a shawl and two little "handkys" last Thursday night and hope you get them safely. I hope my Auntie won't get the hump but really I cannot think of anything for her but feathers and they are very scarce just now. I'll endeavour to get some before leaving here. The pick of them are sent to London direct. The shawl, I am told, is real silk from Japan, and sold at 8s. here and the two handkys cost 1s 8d. I don't know if I've been bit, but certainly I'm not the only one out here to be 'gulled'. When I bought them, I was desperate and only just managed to catch the X'mas Mail with five minutes to spare. It has been the worry of my life sending cards etc., last week and I dare say now that there will be great dissatisfaction all round. However, I haven't much money coming in out here and I'm broke at present. I have had my face taken by a fine photographer here and they are costing me 4/-. I've never been photo'd so much before, but everybody has the craze and we have to be in fashion. I don't get much money to spend on grub, but I'm always hungry and can tackle the rations we get issued to us. My Auntie will find no difficulty in feeding me when I get back. It would do you good to be out here.

It is Dec. now and the weather is at its best. Yesterday morning the temperature dropped as low as 58 in the shade and we were all perished with cold. Ernie Shaw was on Duty from 6 to 8 and when I relieved him at 8 his lips were blue and he was shivering like billyho! I had my waistcoat and tunic on and then could not get warm. It reaches 98 in the middle of the day and we are glad of the warmth. The natives suffer very much from the cold and come into Barracks wrapped up in all kinds of sheets and blankets and Goodness knows what.

Your letters are fine and some of the little bits amuse the Barrack Room greatly. There are lots of blokes out here who have accounts outstanding like Bob what's-his-name. I suppose Harold will have to whistle for his money. I think we as a nation are getting on our backs when the two seedy youths who hang about over the road, have been taken on. The one with the goggles doesn't look very aggressive, does he? I believe that Harold Moxon went hoping he would be rejected. He has stood back as long as possible and has been let in for it at the finish. I suppose Winnie will have been and gone before this letter reaches you but I hope you remembered me to her and that she enjoyed herself whilst at M/c.

Our Platoon lost again on Saturday 2-1. The goal-keeper let us down. He is the Lieutenant in command of our Platoon and let two simple shots through. He was most apologetic to me after the match. I told him that it was a thankless job being a Goal-keeper as a mistake meant a goal. Had it been anybody other than an Officer, I might not have been so sympathetic. Still it was a very good clean game and everybody admitted that we were unlucky in not possessing a good Goalie. I am still retaining the Captaincy and am playing up to form. There's nothing to write about this week. Tell my Auntie that she need not worry about me taking on anything else. As soon as this war is over, I'm done with the Army and Foreign Service.

We Recruits are beating the Trained Men hollow at shooting. I have 110 rounds allowed me to blaze away in firing my course. 110 is a handsome allowance for each man. It's fine shooting. I could do it until further orders. The kick of the rifle is nothing if you hold it properly. A lot of blokes have got bruised shoulders and jaws but I think they must be afraid of their rifles. There is a deal of lead wasted in the Rapid Firing. A lot get the 15 shots off in the minute but never hit the target. 4 seconds is not long to load, get a good sight, pull the trigger, make a pause to retain your sight and then unload. We fire at a Figure Target and the figure looks no bigger than your fore-sight at 500. Well, I'll finish later in the week so ta. ta. for to-night. I am sending a copy of the Musketry Tests. I have been picked to play for our Batt'n to-morrow against the Artillery. I am getting off duty. I'm sending an odd photo which Ernie has by him. I cannot get him to take a decent one of me although I am often posing for him. He is doing a roaring trade with his camera.

I am about bunkered now so will finish before tea. Am dropping a line to Teddy. Hope my Auntie will continue to write, also my Uncle, and of course you must stick it. Well ta. ta. for this week. I'm still in the pink of condition and ready to play tennis with the best man in Stretford. With heaps of love to my Auntie, Uncle, Harold and all at home.

> I remain,
> Your loving little brother
> Matt   xxxxxxxxx

[Annexe to Letter 12]

Regular Army Standard Test - 2nd Course

Possible Scores	Shot	Target	Distance Yards	Rounds	Instruction for conduct of shots
25	Grouping	2nd class Bull's Eye	100	5	Lying
15	Snapshooting	Figure (Silhouette)	200	5	Lying behind cover, Bayonet fixed, 4 seconds each shot.
20	Slow	Figure	400	5	Lying, firing round cover, no rest.
20	Slow	Figure	300	5	Kneeling, taking cover behind wall and firing over it. No rest.
45	Rapid	Figure	300	15	Lying, rifle to be loaded & 4 rounds in magazine before the target appears loading from pouch one minute allowed to fire all the 15 rounds.
20	Slow	Figure	500	5	Lying 30 seconds allowed
20	Rapid	Figure	500	5	" " (Bayonet fixed)
20	Slow	Figure	600	5	" " Taking cover

Note:- The effect of the bayonet being fixed will be to bring the bullet 3 feet down and 12" to the right. By sighting the rifle at 450 yds and aiming 12" to the left this can be overcome at 300 yards.

Scores of 130 and over are Marksmen
Scores of 105 "   "   1st Class Shots and carry 6d a day extra pay.
Scores of 75 "   "   2nd "   "

Ten points are being allowed to Territorials

Letter 13 - 16th December 1914

My dear Uncle,

I have just come from the Gymnasium. I have been picked for our Bayonet Fighting Team in the Competition and we played the 1st round this afternoon. We won 5-3 and have passed into the 2nd Round. There is 8 men from each Platoon and a Cup and Money Prizes to be won. I knocked my man out this afternoon and won the match 2-1. We then played a team, that had got a bye, and beat them. There are 16 of us now representing the whole Double Coy. of 250 men. It's a fine game but rather dangerous. I've got my thumb knocked up. We are firing again this week. Ted Harrison went on the Range yesterday and made the top score, 39 out of 45. I go up to-morrow and Friday and hope to do well.

I have been footballing with a vengeance lately. I'm more like a Professional Footballer. Our Platoon played the top team on Monday and lost 3-0. The match is under protest, however. Yesterday, I was picked to play for the Double Coy. Team against "D" Coy and we won 1-0. Talk about excitement! There was about 500 on the touch line shouting themselves hoarse. The Major has made us a present of the jerseys we played in, as a reward for winning. I've played in some colours since coming here. I've played for the Platoon, the single Coy. team, the Double Coy., and the Battalion and they have a different jersey for each team. We only play 30 minutes each way and generally kick-off at 4-30. The first half hour is terrific but from 5 o'clock to 5-30 it gets nice and cold. I was playing tennis last Friday afternoon with a lot of Sergeants. I seem to have something on every afternoon and so am not tempted to have a sleep. Ernie Shaw and I generally get into bed soon after 8 o'clock every night tired out. It is awfully cold when we get up at 5 o'clock and we are shivering until 8 o'clock. Sometimes the Major lets us pile arms and have a run round. In the middle of the day, it gets as hot as ever.

The opinion seems to be that we will leave here early in February for Marseilles but of course fresh rumours are current every week. Yesterday morning Ernie Shaw and I were marking on the Range. By jove! The bullets don't half whistle thro' the targets. It gives you an idea of being under fire and it's not very pleasant. I wouldn't mind standing up to some of our "crack" shots. Three of them had clean targets at 200 yards. I don't know how they manage it. I wrote to Teddy last week and hope that he is going on alright.

The Germans don't seem to be meeting with much success, and we should be having them on the run very shortly. I hope we get a chance of being in at the kill. One of the junior Lieutenants gave a fine Lecture on the "European crisis." He gave a champion address on the circumstances leading up to the War and showed us how we were in honour bound to throw in our lot with the Allies. This week we have started having an extra ½ lb. of bread on payment of 1¼ a day. With the extra 3d a day we will be feeding well. It is X'mas Day a week on Friday and we have £19 to pay for extras for our Coy. It's our turn to find all the Guards for X'mas week so some of us might have to spend X'mas Day on Guard. I hope you all have good X'mas at home. This letter will reach you after the festivities are over. I'll make up next year for all I've missed. I sent two photos of myself last Saturday and hope they have arrived safely. Ernie Shaw is going strong with his Camera. I cannot afford to buy many photos from him but when we get back, I'll borrow the films and print what I want. He's charging a piastre a print, which is 2½. I'm sending one taken in the Barrack Room. The father of the fellow with the drum lives at Carnarvon and is a J.P. I didn't get a letter from you by last Thursday's Mail and there were no letters for us on Sunday. However I'm looking for a lot of letters to-morrow night.

One of our pals was taken before the Orderly Room for insolence to a Corporal. Five of us went as witnesses for the defence and the Corporal lost the case. The punishment is 48 hours Cells but the five of us stuck out that the Corporal was not insulted (as indeed he wasn't) and we won the case. It is up to us now to give that Corporal no chance of getting at us.

Thursday afternoon. The post goes at 4-30 so I must hurry along with this letter. I was on the Range this morning and did not do so badly. I would have had a fine score if I'd been more careful. At 600 yards I forgot to clamp the sight up and it slipped down 50 yards. We are only on the Qualification Practices as yet and start firing for the extra 6d. next week. The wind is awfully gusty in the early morning out here. At times we have to allow 5 feet of wind. At shooting all the Recruits are mopping the floor with the other blokes. Last week the first 8 on the list were Rookies, I being one of them. I'll put you through it with that air-gun when I get back.

The Mail comes in to-night and if there is not a letter from you, there will be trouble. Mr. Lockwood's father has sent a consignment of 70 books for our Battn. It's very good of him, isn't it? I've been helping Ted Harrison to catalogue them. Ted is in charge of the Library and Billiard Room as I may have told you before. I've nothing much to write about this time so will chuck it. I hope you are feeling well and fit. I believe young Rawcliffe and little Lupton have enlisted, so they may be calling you up, yet. With heaps of love to my Auntie, Cissie and all at home.

I remain,
    your affectionate nephew,
        Matt.

P.S. Remember me to Teddy when you write him. Hope he is still alive and well. He is in the thick of it and I wish him luck.

Letter 14 - 28th December 1914

Khartoum 28 : 12 : 1914

My dear Cissie,

I think it's your turn for a letter so here goes. I've just come from the Range. We've fired the first Practice for the extra Coppers i.e. the Grouping Practice. I was ½ an inch out of an 8 inch group and have been put down as a 12 inch. This is a score of 15 out of the five shots and is, at all events, a good start. It is rough on us having to fire so soon after the X'mas Festivities but it cannot be helped. The English Mail got in on X'mas Eve and I got my letters at 10 o'clock, on coming off duty. It was a record Mail and I was the lucky recipient of ten letters and two papers and the music.

I was on Police Duty last week and during X'mas. There were not many sober on X'mas Eve and the Sergeant of the Police, who was himself perpetually drunk all the week-end, gave us definate instructions to "clink" everybody unruly. The lights didn't go out on X'mas Eve and there wasn't half some fun. The Band was playing all night and all the Sergeants and Officers were also squiffy. The Army, like the Workhouse and other Institutions, makes X'mas Day a day of days. The day's fare, excluding beer ad lib, was as follows: Breakfast, Tinned Rabbit, jam, bread and tea. Dinner:- Steak and Kidney Pie and X'mas Pudding with Sauce (the sauce was to have contained Rum, but the Cooks inadvertently drank the two bottles of Rum thinking they were X'mas presents for them). For tea we had two fancy cakes and a pot of jam between four men. The jam was the best bottled jam obtainable and was fine. The jam we usually get goes under the name of marmalade but resembles Gum Arabic. Well, the day ended up with a Smoking Concert and the beer flowed like water. Of course there were minerals and Cigs. The turn of the evening was the arrival of the Officers, tipsy to a man. They started making speeches and I never enjoyed anything so much before. A good number of our Officers have served in the ranks of the old Mounted Infantry Brigade and the yarns they told of each other had us roaring. There are some really fine speakers amongst our Officers and their tongues were all nice and loose. Most of our blokes were incapable and I put two of them to bed. Well, this ended the noisiest X'mas I have experienced so far and I can tell you, there were some weary bleary eyes blinking at the Reveille next morning. Parades were cancelled for X'mas and Boxing Day but I was on Police Duty unfortunately.

On Sunday we had another full day. Everything seems to happen on Sundays. In the morning we had a Battalion Church Parade and in the afternoon our Company had to turn out on a funeral. A young lad died in Hospital late on Saturday night from Bright's Disease and Double Pneumonia. His name was Kenyon. As you may remember there was a Sergeant named Kenyon who died some time ago but he is no relation to this lad. He was only 18 years of age and his mother had to be persuaded by his brother (who is a Lance-Corporal in our Coy) to let him come out. There was a big turn-out on the Funeral Service and the order of the Procession was as follows. First the Firing Party marching with Butts reversed, then the Brass and Bugle Bands, then the Coffin on an Egyptian Gun Carriage drawn by six white Arab horses, then the bearers and then the Company. We marched to the tune of the Dead March in Saul (as slow as possible.) The Cemetary is 3 miles from the Barracks through Khartoum and tribes of women and kids were following us. At the Cemetary, the Firing Party fired three shots and the bugle band played the Last Post and the grave was filled in. By jove! I prefer Stretford Cemetary to Khartoum Cemetary. The graves are mostly of soldiers who have died here and you can see all the different Regiments who have been stationed out here. We were out from 3 to 6-30 and don't want to go on any more funerals. It must have been awful for the lad's brother seeing him buried in this outlandish place.

The parcel has not arrived yet, nor the X'mas Pudding, but, when they do come, they'll get such a doing. On Wednesday night we are having our Mess feed and amongst other things we've got 3 Turkeys. Each man has paid in 15 piastres (3/-) so we ought to have a bit of something to fly at. This afternoon I was Bayonet Fighting again for our Platoon and we just won 5-4. I beat my man 2 fights against nil and our team is now in the Semi-Final. We have to win the next round and then fight off the Final at the Egyptian Military Tournament of Thursday next before the Sirdar, and all the "Knuts." I'm reading a fine book called the "River War" by Winston Churchill. It is very instructive and gives a good insight into the affairs in the Sudan. You should try to get it from the Library as it makes excellent reading.

A pal of ours has just come back from Sincat. We have 50 of our Company stationed there and they seem to be having a good time. Sincat stands 3,000 feet above sea level and is an important position on the Camel track from Suakin to Abyssinia. The railway crosses the Camel track at Sincat and our men are stationed there to protect it. Sinkat is in the Red Sea Province and the natives are fuzzy-wuzzies and very warlike. They wear their hair like Gollywogs and carry spears and shields about with them always. Our blokes are under canvas at Sinkat and the water supply comes by rail. One night the water tanks were cleaned out waiting for the train with the water. The train went through without stopping and they thought they would die of thirst but next morning a special came from Port Sudan and relieved their anxiety. The railway is of vital importance to all the stations from Port Sudan to Khartoum, and that is why our men are protecting it.

There is a Singing Competition to-morrow night. I have entered both the Sentimental and Humorous Classes and the prize is 1,000 millemes (£1) in each class. They seem to be throwing a lot of money away on Competitions and its time Richardson picked a bit of it up. The audience acts as Judge and I don't know whether my style will suit. There are some awful turns at the Concerts we have but they get applauded to the echo. Two blokes sing Nigger songs in seconds and I could annihilate them. They are worshipped by the audience, however, and are consequently trotted out on every occasion much to our disgust.

Amongst my letters this week, I had one from John Harrison, your Harold, H Shaw, Ma, Auntie and Uncle and I was sitting in the Guard Room until 12 o'clock on X'mas Eve reading them. I will have no end of writing this week and, like you, could do with a Secretary. We get Khedival pay this next week and I must see if I cannot find you something for your birthday. There are heaps of things to buy but the difficulty is in packing and sending them. I hope you got the shawl and bits of nose-rags. I must admit that my taste was a little at fault in regard to colour but will make amends. The photos broke me at the time and I hope you have received them alright.

Ernie Shaw is taking photos on a large scale and I hope to be busy printing some for myself when I return. I will try to send one this week of some kind. It is awfully good of my Uncle trotting about over that parcel and I don't know how to thank him. As he says in his letter, the Co-operative Stores are not exactly promptness personified for I have not as yet heard of the Invoice Note for the Puddin' even. On every parcel a piastre Duty has to be paid and a form signed and countersigned by the Colonel. Mrs Gresham forwarded the X'mas parcels in packing cases and I believe they are in the Customs hands in Khartoum and will be delivered before the New Year, all things being equal.

I hope Teddy is still alright. It must be awful fighting in the frost and snow. I've had a bad leg lately but it is alright now. I got it kicked and cut playing football and the sores festered. I was not off Parades with it but had to have hot fomentations on it every morning. Sores out here take no end of healing and judging by the bandages, you would think our Regiment had been in action. Zinc ointment, black-draughts and Aspirin are dished out wholesale every morning - Zinc ointment for cuts, black-draughts for pains anywhere and Aspirin for everything else, dose usually 10 grains.

Well, I'm now at the end of my tether as regards inspiration so will have to chuck it. Best love to Auntie, Uncle, Ma, your Harold and all in your part of Lancashire. I'm sorry but this letter will have to go round to them all so explain my inability to write to them all this time, there's a dear.

> With heaps of love to you all
> I remain

Your affectionate brother
Thomas Atkins

xxxxxxx

Matt and Cissie.

Letter 15 - 31st December 1914

Dear Everybody,

In the semi-final of the Bayonet Fight, we won 4 matches each and the Leaders (our Sergeant lead our team) had to fight off and we lost. Hard luck being let down by the Sergeant, especially as I have not been beaten. I won every bout.

Immediately after the fight I was waltzed away to play for our Coy. against the R.G.A. and we put up a good game and the result was a goalless draw. I'm just off to the Sudan Military Tournament so 'cuse bad writing.

I have already passed as a 2nd Class Shot but have to score 44 out of the next 15 shots to get the extra 6d. A Second Class Shot only carries 3d a day extra. We have to fire the last three practices and the distances are 500 and 600 yards. The chap named Allan was 10 off being a Marksman. He is a Recruit to this Battn but was a crack shot in the 6th Manchesters.

In haste
Yours to a cinder
Matt.

Letter 16 - 13th January 1915

My dear Cissie,

I received the Registered Parcel on Friday and am delighted with the wristlet watch, which keeps very good time. People are beginning to mistake me for an "Ossifer." The Commander of our Platoon cannot boast anything better than an "Ingersoll" so you see I am amongst the 'Knuts' in regard to timepieces. Your letter was the most remarkable part of the parcel and no kid. After reading of the return of Da,* I must confess that "I'll go to 'L' " was heard to have been uttered by me. I've witnesses to testify that I said it so I stand defenceless. There's no doubt about it but you've "talked him home." I can imagine your disappointment at his appearance in "mufti" and not as an Officer, as you dreamed of him. Dreams never come true to detail. However, you'll no doubt be proud of the "walking records" which your Da has broken on the road from Huddersfield to M/c. Ernie's rude reception was rather too bad just as he reached the winning post. I am rather surprised at my Uncle receiving him with open arms but cannot but admire him for it. He couldn't for the life of him kick a fellow when he's down. I think my Uncle's kindness is as admirable as my Da's "sponging" is despicable. However, you have him on your hands and I cannot imagine what is to become of him. I dare say you have long ago got tired of his dramatic "leg-swinging" descriptions of his adventures since he left us in the autumn a few years back. I suppose he's as proud as "Punch" in the knowledge that his two eldest sons are serving their King and Country. As you say, I'm well out of the fun and although I don't think I could tell him off, it would turn me sick to listen to his yarns. I feel very sorry for you kid, and hope that you soon get him safely off the premises. I dare say he has tried all over to enlist but, as of yore, he's been "too old."Well, I'll now drop the subject and get on to something not so weary.

All this week, we are practicing for the "March Past" and Review by some big General of all the forces in the Sudan.The Review ground is about four miles from Barracks and we went up this morning and are going again on Friday and then on Saturday, which is the day of the Review. It is a long tramp in the sun and at present my legs are as stiff as the collars my Auntie used to "do up."

I was playing footy yesterday for our Coy. against the R.G.A., which might account for some of the stiffness above mentioned. We got a bashing and lost 5-0. My poor nose got into the way of a certain goal for the R.G.A. It's a very funny thing how my nose seems to drop into all the trouble. Candidly, is there anything abnormal about it? There most certainly is at present and for some time to come my handsome "counting house" will be closed to photographers in general. Ernie Shaw's business in photos is reaching astounding proportions and I am seriously thinking of applying for a Clerkship. He is placing orders for printing and developing with the local photographer amounting to 400 or so piastres.There are three photographers in Khartoum and he has a current a/c with each. He has got a fine selection or collection whichever suits the case and I am looking forward to getting the negatives when we get back and printing what I require.

This week the first issue of our Regimental newspaper "The Sentry" was placed before the public and made a tremendous impression throughout Africa. Current editions may not appear for some time as Major Hertz, who is the life and soul of these Competitions, Concerts, etc. was taken bad last Tuesday after giving out the "Bounty" Prizes and was operated upon next morning. He had appendicitis and the operation has turned out satisfactorily. He is an awfully nice chap and unfortunately the paper went to press without being checked by him. Hence the bad grammar and spelling which you will notice in the copy which I am sending. Some of the pithy bits I don't suppose you will fully appreciate, but one or two of the articles are not bad. Dr Morley, the bloke who performed the operation, is very clever with the knife and has performed some wonderful feats with the self-same instrument. The other doctor, Dr Farrer, is an old shaky customer, whom nobody will face if it can be avoided. When he is on duty at the Hospital in the mornings, the attendance is halfed. I was one of the unlucky individuals whom he inoculated and he nearly bowled me over.

I have bought you a Jewel Case, two photo-frames and 6 ivory serveyouright rings and have got them all packed up in a wooden packing case (amongst other things) ready to take to the P.O. tomorrow. I don't know what the postage will be but that don't worry me so much as the forms which I'll have to fill up. I believe you have to declare what the articles are and their value. I believe the authorities can demand an inspection of the goods, which, in addition to me having to open the box, will no doubt reveal the metal jewel-box. All metal, it seems, is "off-side" in War time to use a footballing term. However, I'm living in hopes of "kidding" the Post Office Authorities, which after all is not a hard job. Of course, I don't mean to make any insinuations as to those at Brown St. Far from it. Their reputation is well-known and needs no comment from me. If you should see a lurry drawing up to 91 sometime in the near or far future, don't get alarmed. It is only my packing case. Personally, I am proud of the way I've nailed up this 'ere box. After the hours I've spent on it, I am somewhat reluctant to hand it over to the tender mercies of the Post Office, and, if possible would like to deliver it personally. No! I'm not getting home-sick. Who said I was? All I'm hoping for is that there won't be any disappointment in the division of the spoil, if the beggar ever comes to hand. I bought the photo-frames, ivory rings and jewel case especially for your birthday and had overlooked the fact that it takes at least two years for a parcel to reach you. You will notice that there are three articles - one for each of the three birthdays between now and the parcel reaching you. To be precise, your 36th, 37th and 38th birthdays. In passing, I might say that I've heard nothing as yet of the parcel in the Gresham case nor of the Co-op. Plum Pudding. The Gresham case is said to be on the way and its arrival is patiently being waited for by a good many (including your humble.) A few 'puddin's' came in during last week and they were as green as grass. They looked like balls of green paint and I believe they're fetching a good price at the cheese-mongers. When you are eating your favourite Gorgonzola, kid, just think what a "fake" some of the green may be.

Last Sunday, four of us went to Omdurman and had a very busy day. Sunday here, instead of being the day of rest and tennis as it used to be in Stretford, is the day when we see life. We saw it with a vengeance at Omdurman. We were the only four "soldiers" there that day and the natives took a lively interest in our doings. It's a funny sensation having men, women and kids following you about, as if you were some new species of biped. To use an American phrase or shall I say a Carborundum** phrase, we "did" Omdurman "proper." We visited the house and tomb of the renowned Mahdi or Khalifa which amounts to the same thing. He was supposed to be the New Prophet sent down from Heaven (something like Kaiser Bill only more modest) and was the cause of all the trouble in the Sudan. His house is a fine three-storied building and has a big flat roof, from which he used to review his Dervishes. In some of the rooms are piles of old fire-arms, spears, shields, horse pistols etc., and there is also the remains of a piano, which it is said, Gordon used to play upon previous to his massacre when Khartoum was captured by the Dervishes two days before the Expedition arrived to relieve him. There are also some guns and 5 carriages which the Mahdi captured in Abyssinia and dragged over the desert to Omdurman, a distance of about 3,000 miles. The tomb is in ruins, it having been shelled by the Nile Gunboats and ultimately blown up by Kitchener after Omdurman was taken. The blowing-up of the Mahdi's tomb destroyed Mahdism completely in the Sudan and the natives are now as contented and happy as pigs in warm mud. Every day you can see traces of the Mahdi's atrocities. There are men and women going about with their eyes put out and with legs and hands cut off. In the house there are instruments of torture. He used to issue his own coins and the press is still to be seen in his "beit" which means his house.

Well, after a fierce encounter with the donkey-lads over the fare, we eventually cut them off with a piastre (not a shilling) and went through the markets. Here I got a bargain in the serveyouright rings. They wanted 5 piastres each for them but after a lot of arguing with the fair damsel who was endeavouring, with others, to do business with us, I at length got 6 for 10 p.t. or 2s/1d in English coin. Of course I had to smile sweetly at her and assure her that they were given away in Khartoum. Khartoum used to be a great place for elephants which also means ivory. In fact the name in itself stands for 'Elephant' in Sudanese lingo. You can buy beautiful silver-work but it is too dear altogether. All the work is done by hand and is so minute. It is sold at 3 p.t. a drachm. They seem to have very hazy ideas as to English avoirdupois which one can hardly wonder at. Until only recently the bloke at the Canteen has been giving us 100 lbs of potatoes when we ordered 1 cwt. He naturally thought they were trying to twist him when they told him that there were 112 lbs in a cwt. Of course it most likely in this case was an instance of being not so daft as to learn. For twisting, the Greeks who run our Canteen, can lick Jews into a cocked hat.

The latest news I have left to finish up with. Ernie and I are picked as Signallers, for the Company. Our names were in orders this morning. We are no longer a fighting unit of the Army but act as Scouts, which involves greater dangers. In addition to rifle and equipment we will now have to carry flags and Heliograph apparatus. We don't go out with the Coy. after this week but practice under the Sergeant of Signallers. I can send messages in Semaphore but as yet have not started on the Morse Code.

Well, I seem to have spun out a long letter, much longer than I thought I could manage, and at last have come to the end of my tether. I can't get over the old man turning up again but it hasn't, as yet, spoiled my sleep. I am eagerly looking forward to the Mail on Thursday in the hope of hearing further particulars. He seems to have just timed his visit in time to spend X'mas with you all. I can well imagine Marny bursting out laughing on spying the "swinging leg". When all's said and done it has its humorous side if it were not for the "showing up." I must chuck it now as it is ten to nine by my left wrist and past my bedtime. Give my love to Marney, my Uncle, your Harold and all at home. I suppose you'll be "having the Radihater on" eh? Well "Goodnight Sarah Lizzie."

I remain
Your loving brother
Matt
xxxxxxx

P.S. Marney and my Uncle are both due for a letter and I hope they'll "jump to it" as they say in the Army.

* [Matt's father. See Notes - Extract from the Richardson and Ridley family history.]

** [Matt's younger brother Ernie worked for the Carborundum Company in Trafford Park (Manchester). The company was American owned.]

Letter 17 - 20th January 1915

Khartoum   20/1/1915

My dear Uncle,

I think it is your turn for a letter so here goes. I got a letter from Cissie by Sunday's Mail. I've not, however, had one from you or my Auntie for some time - X'mas Eve in fact. I dare say Cissie, writing as she does at such great length, leaves you no material to write about. I find it an awful job to get something to write about each week but I've kept it up so far and managed to spin out a letter of respectable length.

I will again acknowledge receipt of the wristlet watch, which I find of great service in my new capacity as Signaller, what! what! In future "Sgnlr." and not "Pte." Richardson - nothing so common as "Pte." There are 8 Signallers attached to each Coy. and 32 in all to the Battn. It is a superior job to being in the ranks, although Ernie Shaw and I were both in the running for a stripe had we remained with the Company. We are classed as Details and don't do Guards. There were ten of us picked to make up the full complement of 32 "Waggers." One of the Recruits is "Horrocks" a fellow whom Lily Sands from across the way, knows. He asked us the other morning if we knew her and of course we did. It is marvellous what a lot of fellows one meets in this Batt'n, whom one has met before. There are blokes I used to go to school with, in addition to others I've known by sight for years. We are being trained in Semaphore and Morse Signalling and despatch riding. To carry the despatches we are supplied with bikes but they are practically useless in this country, where there is nothing but sand. We don't get much scope for training for the Continent owing to the nature of the country. For instance, in addition to the flags, we use the heliograph extensively out here, whereas in France it would be of no use through the absence of the sun at this time of the year. You can flash a message out here by the heliograph and it can be read 40 miles away. We have to go through the Classification Test next month. This examination includes map-reading and setting, despatch carrying and sending and receiving messages in Code at 10 words per minute. We will have plenty to occupy our minds for a few weeks and we are putting in a lot of practice.

On Saturday it was the March Past and Review by the Sirdar, Sir Reginald Wingate. The Sirdar was very pleased with our performance and said that we maintained the standard kept us by the Regulars in previous years. When he heard that the "Terriers" were coming to garrison Khartoum, he was naturally very anxious as to the safety of the place but he is now quite satisfied with us and won't let us leave if he can stop us. It was a fine sight to see all the cavalry, artillery and camel corps going past the saluting base at the "Charge" and the marching of the Infantry seemed to fall into quite a tame affair by comparison. In all there were ten Battalions of Infantry marching past in quarter column, consisting of Egyptians, Sudanese and our own Battn. and the native women set up a terrible "Lu-lu"ing as each Company passed. Instead of clapping, the women make a high "Coo-ee"ing noise. They gave our Battn a good ovation as we passed.

On the Sunday the Sirdar invited all our N.C.O.s and men to a Garden Party at the Palace and of course Ernie and your humble were there early, with our boots blacked. We went all over the Palace in parties of from 20 to 30 and had a fine look round. The Sirdar personally showed us through the Library and went to no end of pains explaining the many photographs etc. He was Kitchener's right hand man in the campaign against the Khalifa and was Chief of the Intelligence Dept. He took photos of the battlefield immediately after the capture of Atbara and Omdurman. The battlefields were simply covered with white-robed Dervishes and on one photo all the Khalifa's chief generals and body-guards are lying dead in a group, altho' the Khalifa himself escaped with his life. The Sirdar personally chased him after Omdurman had fallen and eventually ran him to earth at Kordofan 12 months afterwards. The Sirdar is only a short stiff-built chap but he is fine, and treats us all like his own lads. He knows all the different languages spoken in the Sudan and is worshipped by the natives.

There was a lot of grub knocking about but it didn't last long when the 7th Manchesters got loose amongst it. I had five rock buns, tea, lemonade, biscuits etc. and made the most of my time whilst the provisions lasted. He hopes to have us all up again soon. So do I. I am afraid that we will be in Khartoum until next autumn. We fully thought we would get a move this week but it was a "cell." There was an order for the 7th Lancs Fusillers to relieve the 7th Man. on the 18th of this month. It turned out that it was our detachment at Alexandria who were being relieved and not us. General Douglas is coming down to inspect us on the 20th of next month, so we won't leave till then at all events. If we stay after February, they cannot bring any troops to relieve us till the following October as they cannot come to Khartoum in the summer, owing to the heat.

When we went to Omdurman the other Sunday, we got talking to a Sergeant Instructor to the Sudanese Army. Both the Egyptian and Sudanese Instructors are English and they have good jobs training these native troops. This bloke is attached to the Engineers - Post & Telegraph section. He has been out here four years and is a very steady chap, being a non-smoker and teetotaller. They get free board and lodging and he says he can save £3 a week. During last summer, he said, there were two of their Instructors being carted to the Cemetary every week through heat stroke but they were chiefly fellows who drank a lot of beer and whiskey during the heat of the day. You see the alcohol causes their temperature to rise and then with the heat getting up to 120 degrees they were soon bowled over. This chap was fixing up Wireless Apparatus at Omdurman or he would have showed us round.

Last Saturday, I took the package mentioned in full detail in last week's letter, to the Post Office. After filling in two forms, I succeeded in getting it taken over the counter without opening it for 12 piastres - 2s/6d. I hope it arrives at Cromwell Rd some time this year. I might say that the parcel you went to so much trouble over has not yet come up to scratch. The Gresham Case seems to be a myth. Some say it is at Alexandria, others at Port Sudan, but all agree that it is on the way. The CWS Pudding is also on the way and may arrive in time for next X'mas. I believe they improve with keeping but hope that it won't be green by the time it gets here. You don't appear to have received a couple of Photos which I posted well in time for X'mas. I am sending a Postcard in case the mounted P.O.'s have gone astray. Enclosed also find a snap taken at the Sudan Military Tournament. I am playing against the Fort this afternoon.

On Friday there is a Regatta on the Nile and I am entering one of the rowing events. The Colonel last night at the weekly Concert seemed to be rather downhearted about the affairs on the Continent. He said our Artillery was far inferior to that of the Germans but that we far excelled them in Infantry. It seems that the trenches are in some cases as near as 40 yards apart and that the battlefields are absolutely deserted and not a human being to be seen. It's a funny way of fighting and our training seems to have been all wrong. There's no doubt about it, but we're in Paradise here compared to the conditions at the Front. It seems that, according to the German Press, Khartoum has fallen and the Turks have simply wiped the floor with the British Garrison. I'm very sorry to hear it. I wish they would come near Khartoum. We would get a bit of excitement then and be able to say we'd done something for our grub.

I must chuck it now. With heaps of love to Marny, Cissie, her Harold, all at home and Tommy.

I remain
Your loving nephew
Matt

P.S. Hope you and my Auntie are keeping well. From all accounts, people will have to keep their umbrellas up if they don't want to be hit by bombs from Zeppelins. Don't forget to write soon.

Letter 18 - 1st February 1915

Khartoum 1st Feb. 1914
Monday

My good people

I have just finished a bit of "natty" sewing and in the interval between now and 4-30 (when I am playing football) I am writing this letter. There was no English Mail in last Thursday nor yet on Sunday for what reason I don't know. We are all hoping for one coming in on Thursday. I have just finished the cake. It kept fine, and with the chocolate and what not, I have had a birthday all week. I don't feel like writing this afternoon so will chuck it and get ready to play football. I believe this is absolutely the last time I shall turn out this season. Let's hope that next season, I'll be in a more suitable climate for football. I'm chucking it now.

(Tuesday afternoon Feb 2nd)

Here I am again. We won yesterday 3-0 against No. 15 Platoon and are justly proud of our performance. I have got a nice black-eye. I was heading the ball as one of the other team was kicking it. Hence the black-eye! However, I won't grumble as the other day I gave a bloke out of our Mess a beautiful eye. It's been all the colours of the rainbow. We started sparring and it turned out to fighting. I finished up the scrap with landing him one right in the eye and it swelled up in no time. Of course I was sorry and I dare say he is. At the Institute this afternoon I am playing in the 1st Round of the Tennis Tournament. There is an entry of 40 players and there are some very good tennis heads amongst them. I have bumped up against one of the "Knuts" right away. I play a chap out of the R.A.M.C. named Crompton. He is a dentist from Bolton and can pull out teeth in fine style. Let's hope he cannot play Tennis as well as he can "yank" ivories out. One of the chaps who has entered is the Amateur Champion of Cheshire and he is practically a "cert."

I've been working overtime on the bathing lately. It's the only place where you can get cool. Somebody has told us that we'll get Nile rash so now after every time we've been in, we all go with all speed and have a bath in Condy's Fluid. Of course, I don't think that there is anything in the water to hurt you but its best to be on the safe side. The natives drink the Nile water by the gallon and are glad to get it. Our doctor reckons that if we drink a pint of it we would certainly get Dysentry. Ernie Shaw has taken some fine photos and I'll send as many as I can this mail.

Our Signalling Examination comes off in 2 or 3 weeks and then we, most probably, will get scattered about a bit. We have detachments of the 7th at Port Sudan, Sincat, Atbara and Sobat and it is usual to have communication between these stations by heliograph. The Camel Corps is at Sobat, which is about 15 miles out of Khartoum and their 'helio' can be read with a naked eye with ease. Both the British and Egyptian Camel Corps are at Sobat grazing the camels. In a short time, they are going on a long "trek" of about 700 miles. There are a lot of natives in the interior of the Sudan, who don't yet know that there is a War on and of course they have to be told. The Turks don't get much sympathy from the people of the Sudan.

It was the Sudanese X'mas last week and Prayer Meetings and other Festivities were held in Khartoum. It is a grand place for 'Xmases'. There is the Egyptian X'mas, our own, and the Sudanese. There seems to be something going on in Khartoum every week during the season. It's not much but it is something. I believe Khartoum gets quite a lot of visitors during January but this year, owing to the War, it is more or less deserted. The curio-shops in Omdurman are very slack in consequence and it is a good chance of getting something on the cheap. I may go again on Sunday if it keeps fine.

Our blokes haven't half been going through it all last week and this week. They've been trench digging from 6 in the morning until getting on for 11 o'clock. The trenches are elaborate in the extreme, with barbed wire entanglements and head cover, sleeping compartments and communication trenches all complete. They are about 4 miles out and I believe that they have been constructed for the Fort to practice blowing them up. I understand that we are to watch the effect of shell-fire from about 500 yards off where the shells burst. They've been rushing the job through as quick as possible and I think that it is really a precautionary measure. 7 out of our Coy. have come back with injuries and you'd think to look at them, that our Battn had been in action. They've been working too close together and have been belting one another with the pickaxes.

There is an amateur performance of "Eliza comes to stay" at Khartoum this week and I intend to go to-night. Two of our Officers are taking small parts in it. The Sudanese Military Band are responsible for the music. The show starts at 9-15 and we are allowed passes up till 12. o'clock. The charges are 50 and 25 p.t. civilians and 5 p.t. troops. I'm absolutely bunkered now so will chuck it and finish later.

Wednesday night

Here I am again. I have just come off Parade. It is turned 9 and I have about an hour before "Lights Out" to do a little scratching. We have just received the most cheering news that there won't be an English Mail in until a week next Thursday. Rotten, ain't it? The reason of the delay I think is on account of the Suez Canal being unsafe for the mail boats. They call at Port Sudan and then go down to Durban as a rule but perhaps owing to the hostilities with Turkey, they have to go round the Cape of Good Hope and up again to Port Sudan. That may or may not be the solution but the fact remains that there has been no mail for 3 weeks. I hope our letters are reaching England safely. I write regularly every week so don't get alarmed if they fail to arrive as regularly.

To-morrow we are having a big Field-day. Reveille at 4-30 and we then proceed to attack those trenches in co-operation with the Garrison Artillery. We have to advance under the Artillery fire and eventually deliver the assault with the bayonet. Our Machine Guns are also firing at them and we are blazing away real stuff. It will be a novel experience and give us an idea of Artillery fire. The gunners smash the trenches up with Lyddite and then fire shrapnel. The Lyddite is terrible and smashes up the trenches something awful and is supposed to dislodge the enemy. They then fire shrapnel to scatter them after they have left the trenches. I don't know yet what part we (the Flag-waggers) will take but perhaps it will be signalling to the Fort and "Cease Fire" etc.

Last night I went the pace and no error. I played my round in the Tournament and lost 2 sets to 1. I put up a very good show and was satisfied with my defeat. Crompton should go a long way in the tournament. I haven't had much practice whereas all the R.A.M.C. play regularly on a court belonging to the nurses. I went to the Gaiety afterwards with Pieterson and 5 others and it was a fine show. I didn't get to bed till 1 o'clock this morning and I had to be up again at 5. I can hardly keep my peepers open but will stick it a bit.

We've got a bloke in Hospital who has gone mad and things are a bit lively. He is an ex-soldier on the staff at the War Office at Khartoum and his son committed suicide some little while back and it has turned his brain. We have to have a Guard on him and last night he was shouting and raving all night through. To-day he stripped himself stark naked, put his clothes through the bars and proceeded to break up his bed and everything in his padded room. All day long he keeps up a conversation with the Sirdar, Kitchener and other notabilities. He is being moved to Cairo out of the heat shortly and the sooner he goes the better as he can be heard all over the Barracks shouting 'Form Fours' and other comments when he is not holding conversations with different people. He is a fine big chap and it is an awful pity. The temperature reaches 103 degrees yesterday in the shade and it now will get hotter until the end of May.

I believe the Colonial Territorial troops are in action with the Turks in the Sinai Peninsula. It is just our luck being out of it. The latest rumour as to our movements is that the Girl Guides are coming to relieve us while we go and join our Division at Cairo. Personally I fancy the Salvation Army are as likely to relieve us as anybody. I'm afraid we're booked here for the summer, worse luck. I can't write any more tonight so will finish off this letter to-morrow. So Goodnight everybody.

Thursday (2-5 by my wrist).

This morning we finished one phase of the attack on the trenches. The Blue Army (or the enemy) is supposed to have driven us into Khartoum last night and early this morning we went out to meet them. They erected iron targets in the sand to represent the Van Guard of the enemy and we were firing at them from 600 yards off. The Artillery were directing their fire on the Main Body in the trenches. They got the Range in the 3rd shot. It was very strange but it was misty this morning. Consequently there wasn't much to see. The weather is hotter now than is usual for the time of the year. It gets to 103 degrees whereas the temp. for the corresponding time last year was only 87½ degrees.

I am sending a lot of prints this week, as they are so good. I hope you won't blush. Our Major is a "demon" at Lacrosse and I'm having a game on Saturday. He has brought about 24 bats out with him, and I've got one to practice with. One of our Officers, Lieut. Whitley, is the best First Home in England and plays in the international games. It seems a decent game and is chiefly adaptable to good runners.

It now is current that there is a Mail in to-night. We are living in hope. I must chuck it now. Heaps of luv to all at home, Uncle, Auntie, Cissie, Harold, Tommy etc. etc. I hope that Teddy is still sticking it. I expect the Germans will get a bashing when Kitchener's new Armies get into the field. We are eagerly watching the Reuters each day but they only contain the same old story. Nothing doing, merely holding. Hoping that you are all fit and well as I am.

I remain
'Thomas Atkins Jun'r'
xxxxxxxxx

Letter 19 - 15th February 1915

Khartoum, Sudan
15/2/1915

My dear Uncle,

Cissie's was the only letter I received by Sunday's mail but I'm glad to say that, as usual, it was one of an exhaustive nature. I also got two papers and "She only started giggling" enclosed with one of them. I don't know whether I've omitted to acknowledge them or not, but I've got papers about every other week since I've been here. I don't get much chance of reading them, however. We get confused reading papers of all dates, as the current news comes through in Reuters Telegrams and then we read about it three weeks afterwards in the papers. There is a telegram every day from London, Paris, St Petersburg, Vienna, Rome or wherever there is anything exciting going on. Of late, they haven't been worth reading, as things seem to be at a stand-still. I suppose we'll be hearing things when our new Armies get going. It doesn't look as though we are being relieved. The Sirdar, our Hon. Col., is inspecting the Barracks and men on Saturday and we have been busy cleaning up for his arrival. Talk about Spring-cleaning, it isn't in it? I'll be able to turn to navvying or anything when I get back. We made our exit from the Medal Competition last Thursday, after reaching the Semi-Final. We had hard lines and lost 2-0. Had we won, we would have been certain of a medal as there are two sets given.

I'm sorry I've never thought of wearing Ted Harrison's dark spectacles till Cissie suggested it. However, I've no doubt all the team will buy them to play in and things will go well if they don't get smashed. The sun is certainly very glazing but nobody has had the cheek to turn out in smoked glasses. I'm seriously thinking of going round Khartoum in them singing "I am but a Poor Blind Boy." We have to play again to-morrow and I think that will finish our footballing programme for this season. The Fort finished playing two weeks ago and it certainly is getting too hot. After a game of football, I feel fairly fresh, which shows I am getting used to the climate and in form. I have Captained our Platoon in every match, in addition to playing regularly in the Double Coy. and Battn Matches. Exercise is the only way to keep fit, for me at all events.

I'll tell you what! You might get Cissie to get me the words of some of George's Humorous Recitations as the Concerts out here are getting "stale" and I should like to give something fresh. "How we saved the barge" and some like that. They must be glaringly funny or else they won't be appreciated by our blokes. Most turns, which would make old women and the like roar with laughing, don't get a smile out here. I don't think "Giggling" will take very well. It seems a bit above them. You would have laughed the other night. A chap sang "The Floral Dance" without the accompaniment and he didn't half "get the bird." I felt sorry for him as it would have been very decent with a good piano accompaniment. When it came to the last chorus in the octave, there wasn't half a howl. The accompaniment, as Cissie and Harold will agree, is the best part of the song. I am glad to hear that John Green is "bucking up" a bit. It's funny he hasn't had a letter from me yet. I wrote him a long one at X'mas time.

We are having a photograph taken of the Signallers with the Colonel, Adjutant and our Officer. There are 32 Signallers in all, 8 being attached to each Company when the Battalion goes into action. If we are destined to stay here for the summer, we are to go up to Sincat for two months training. I'm hoping we go as Sincat stands 3000 feet above sea-level and the mountainous district will give us splendid facilities for signalling and carrying messages. The Scouts come out with us, and together it will make a nice party of about 50. I think I've said something about Sincat in a previous letter. It's in the Red Sea Province and on the Camel Track from Suakin to Abyssinia. It will be a change from here although we will be isolated and have to rough it somewhat. Our detachment, which has been stationed there for a few months, has gone up to Port Sudan. The natives out there in the mountains are different to those round here, and are called Fuzzy-Wuzzies.

You would hardly think it but the Sudan has a History. The Principal from the Gordon Training College in Khartoum gave us a Lecture on the Sudan the other night and it was very interesting. It's as old as Egypt and the people from Egypt used to raid the Sudan and bring back slaves. There is no doubt that these Ethiopians from the Sudan built the Pyramids. Most of the history has come to light recently. An American Professor has recently been excavating round Dongola, which isn't far from here and, amongst other things, he opened out some large mounds, like mole-hills on a very large scale. These turned out to be tombs of big "Knuts" who were without doubt Egyptians. The corpse is laid on a bed with gold and other precious ornaments and around the corpse, all his wives and slaves are entombed alive. Of course, there are numerous inscriptions etc., round about and I've no doubt that the wives in those days were more than sorry when their husbands died. The Professor was under the impression that the wives and slaves must have been drugged before being buried as, in only one case, did they find evidence of any contortion. This may have been a case where the drug had not acted. In one case as many as 500 were buried with one corpse, who was one of the Egyptian Princes. The people from the Sudan were and are still a long-lived race. They never appear to grow older and live well over a century. It was a very interesting lecture and the Professor went through the history of the Sudan, very roughly of course, from about 3000 B.C. to about 400 A.D. They appear to have been a very intellectual people in those days and to have had very noble aspirations and feelings, the latter especially in regard to animals, especially horses.

Major Hertz is the life and soul of the social side of our Battn and since he has been ill, things have fared badly. However, he has got well over his operation for Appendicitis and on Saturday another issue of "The Sentry" is being published for circulation throughout Africa. He is a Barrister in M/c and there was an article in one of the M/c papers about our paper and a letter of appreciation of our efficiency by the Sirdar, our Hon. Colonel. Did you see it?

We are still working hard at Signalling and go out every other night dispatch- running. Last Friday we had a night out. We were in the trenches all night. You know those trenches about 3 miles out into the desert. Well, we fell in at 8 o'clock and proceeded out to the trenches. Our Company were defending the position whilst "D" and "C" Companies were attacking us. Our Company marched out with full pack and occupied the position. We posted outposts, pickets and sentries and those who were not for Duty got into the trenches. Luckily, I was not for Duty so I got into a trench and made myself at home. They are fine large trenches. Over 6 feet deep and there are loop-holes and head cover. You step onto a ledge to fire. There are communication and rest trenches and everything is quite comfortable. The ground is like granite and it was an awful job digging them out. In the front were erected wire entanglements and I put my rifle through my loophole, trained it and loaded it, put my greatcoat on and went to sleep beautifully at the bottom of the trench. We were firing blank cartridge and should the alarm have been given, I would only have had to get up on the ledge and fire. There was no alarm but we stood to arms at 4 o'clock. It was lovely to see the sun rise and with the sun came the enemy. After a few shots, the outposts and sentries came running in and took up their positions in the trenches and we prepared to receive the enemy. Ours was the centre of the position but they went round the wire entanglements. The Major despatched a squad of us out to cut off the enemy's retreat. This we did, and took a lot of prisoners. It was a bit of a "mix-up." We were dashing about with fixed bayonets, blazing away on all sides. It's not a joke fighting in full pack, I can assure you. We're used to skirmishing in drill-order without our valise, haversack, water bottle and entrenching tool and we find it a bit heavier when we get all on and ammunition. We got back at 8 o'clock for breakfast and had to clean up for C/O's inspection at 9-30. Blank cartridge makes a terrible mess of your barrel. It gave us a good idea of life in the trenches but of course there was no wet. It seems a pity, but the Fort were firing at them yesterday and made a mess of them. They will be easy to make up again if they are required, however.

It is no use sending any more parcels as we have to pay 5 p.t. or so on them. With what you pay on postage in addition it makes them very expensive. In addition, we will move shortly, if we are going to move at all. It's rather a forlorn hope, I fear. I must chuck it now as I'm bunkered. I got a nasty mosquito bite on Sunday but nothing has come of it as yet. It's very sore but I put Iodine on it immediately and it seems to be all right. It was a big beggar and it got down my shirt and gave me a nasty sting. It pegged out after emptying itself in me. They cause Malaria if not attended to at once. I'm chucking it now. With love to my Auntie, Cissie, Harold and all at home.

I remain

Your affectionate nephew

Matt

P.S. Write soon. Remember me to Ted when you write him.

P.P.S. My Auntie is getting behind in her letter-writing. I don't half miss the poetry. Tell her to mind the Zeppelins, and always keep her "gamp" up. Ta. ta. till next week.

Unidentified photo from Matt's collection – the building is the Sirdar's Palace in Khartoum.

Letter 20 - 20th March 1915

No 2263 'A' Coy
1/7th Manchester Regt
Khartoum, Sudan
20th March, 1915

My dear Uncle,

I got only a short letter on Sunday from Cissie. The mail goes at 4 o'clock this afternoon and it is now 2-30 so I have not much time to think of much to write. I mounted Guard on Tuesday afternoon and did not come off till last night and this has put me behind in my correspondence. It was terribly hot on Guard and I was not sorry to come off, I can tell you. The hot weather has started with a vengeance. It has been up to 108 degrees in the shade all last week and this. Yesterday it reached 109.2 so you can see that we are not exactly shivering. The wind has a lot to do with the unpleasantness. During the three Winter months just passed the wind blows from the North and it is a cooling breeze. The wind now blows from the South and it is hot. It comes from the Equator across endless tracks of sand and it seems to scorch everything up. I don't know what Hell is like, but if it's worse than Khartoum in the summer, I'm not going there and I should not advise anybody else to go. The Nile is cool but unfortunately we have been prohibited to bathe therein on account of "crocs" and the possibility of getting fever. We have any amount of shower-baths but the water gets warm going through the pipes. The water supply comes from wells dug in the sand and although it has a flavour, it is quite safe to drink as much as possible. We are advised to wallow in it so it must be good "moyer" as it is called here. We keep it in big earthenware jars called "Zears." When the water is put in, it is warm but in a few hours it gets quite cold. As you know, water jars have been in vogue in Egypt since the days of Pharaoh so they are an old established institution and a worthy one. I don't know what the cooling process is, but I believe the porous nature of the earthenware both purifies and cools the water.

I sent two large photographs off last week, one of the Signallers and the other of our Platoon. It was rather expensive sending them separate so a lot of the blokes in the "Waggers" suggested that we sent them all in a big parcel to the Y.M.C.A. Scouts to be delivered from their place in Manchester. My two photos have been sent addressed to Cissie so if you see a bare-kneed Boy Scout toddling up our walk, you'll know that he has come with the photos above referred to. It would cost at least 6 pt. to send the photographs singly as the packing costs a good deal. One of the "Waggers" used to be a Scoutmaster and he says that his Boy Scouts will be only too pleased to do any little job of this sort. They are very useful, aren't they? When we were confined to the Shed at Burlington St., they were kept quite busy running errands. Their chief beauty lies in the fact that they don't expect "tips." Niggers want "backsheesh" as they call it for every little job they do. By the way, never say that anybody "works like a nigger." It's all wrong! You never saw a nigger working at top pressure in your life and they never hurry unless somebody is behind them encouraging them with a stick or something heavy and persuasive. However, it is not to be wondered at that people have not much energy in this part of the world as the heat makes one quite listless. From 12 to 4 everybody are inside their bungalows and the barrack square is deserted. We lay on our beds with nothing on but a little pair of knickers and thank our luck that we are not on Guard. Even laying on our bunks, we get wet through with perspiration, but when we have to go on Guard in the sun with long pants, tunics, equipment, ammunition and rifle, it's enough to crease a bloke. When you come off after doing a 2 hour shift, you feel like a wet dish-cloth. The sweat comes through your tunic even.

I am sending a snap of the Cathedral and also a photo of No. 2 Platoon reduced to Postcard size. It is a poor photo. It's a ¼ plate taken off a full plate and not up to much.

Stan Newbould was carted into Hospital the other night with pains in his stomach and he has only just escaped Appendicitis. He has been troubled with pains in his "Little Mary" since we came here. He wears one of those abominable belts and I think that that may have something to do with the trouble. We still have cases of Malaria and Dysentry. Our Major Hertz, the Editor of "The Sentry" unfortunately has been invalided home and we are all most sorry to lose him. He was the life and soul of the social events in our Barracks and I don't know what will become of the newspaper in his absence. Some of our Sergeant Instructors left to rejoin their Regiments and the others will be going shortly. A lot of our chaps have applied for Commissions and got them. It is the latest way of "working your ticket" as they say in the Army, which means getting discharged and sent home. I believe they are only temporary Commissions and by the time one gets home and is attached to some Regiment I should imagine that the War will be over. We have just heard of the sinking of the "Dresden." The Telegrams we get are still of the same variety i.e. "We repulsed etc and gained 100 yards of trenches etc." I think they are only nibbling until they get all our forces in the field and then there will be something on the Reuters one way or another. In the meantime, we have to stick it out here and sweat.

I'm sending this letter without a stamp as the Adjutant informs us that we are out here on Active Service now since Turkey came into the War. I hope you'll give me all news of Teddy when you write. The weather will not be so severe now, will it? I would give anything to get drenched to the skin in some real English rain. I'll bet Longford Park is now getting green again. It's like Autumn here. The leaves are all falling off. The Summer here is like Winter as it scorches everything up and nothing can grow.

I've nothing much to write about this week so I hope you'll excuse such a short letter. It gets too blooming hot during the afternoon even to think.

Last Sunday we had a Battalion Church Parade to the Cathedral. We got there like a lot of drowned rats, sweating out of every pore. The heat bursted the skins of two side-drums. Our brass band plays for the Service and has created a fine reputation in Khartoum and district. They get lots of engagements at various places. Our Bugle

Band however, has suffered badly through the heat. Nearly all the Buglers have cracked lips and when the bugles get hot, pandemonium reigns. I went to the Cathedral again on Sunday night. It's a fine photo I'm sending this week. You cannot go far wrong out here with a pretty rapid Lens. Ernie Shaw has got hundreds of fine films and I'll be working overtime on them when I get back, printing off them.

I must now chuck it as the Postman is off. So with heaps of luv to Marny, Cissie, her Harold, Ma, Ernie, Rid and Harold and Tommy,

I remain,
Your loving nephew
Matt

P.S. You seem to be getting my letters alright every week. Yours come very irregularly. When I expect a few, I get none and when I least expect them, I get a batch of them. Newspapers must get lost on the way as I very rarely get them.

Unidentified photo – possibly by the Nile at Khartoum.
The central figure wearing a helmet may be Matthew Richardson.

Letter 21 - 23rd March 1915

Khartoum, Sudan

23rd March 1914 (Tuesday afternoon)

My dear big Sister,

No Mail came into Khartoum last Thursday bu[t] on Sunday I received a letter from you. I am very sorry to hear that my Auntie and Uncle have both been ill and hope that long before this reaches you, they are better. I should think the weather will be getting much warmer now. Have you had a severe Winter? Was there any skating? I'll bet Longford Park is looking green again. How is our garden going on? Has anything been done in regard to extending the Tennis Court? I hope to be home in time to move the hedge back for next year, if it has not already been moved. I suppose there will be more Hens than ever on the Tennis Courts this season.

All sport is stopped for the Summer in the Sudan on account of the heat. The glass was up and down last week. It rose steadily to 109.4 degrees in the shade, next day the maximum temperature was only 98 degrees and the next day it dropped to 87 degrees. It all depends upon the wind. It is very hot again to-day on account of the South wind. Next month the South wind brings with it sand-storms. Then for April, May, June, July, August and Septr it is as hot as "L" all over the Sudan.

We have suspended all training now and our work now consists of Guards, Fatigues when required and light Swedish drill. Wednesday in the Sudan is a general holiday for the Troops stationed there and we started it last Wednesday, (when I was on Guard). We would have had all Wednesdays off ever since coming here had not Turkey stepped into the War. For the first three months of our time in Khartoum, things were desperately serious. We were slogging away with our training and the R.G.A. at the Fort were working night and day Sundays included making ready for all emergencies. You see, both the Sudanese and Egyptians are Mohammedans and if Turkey's intervention had been taken as a Religious War, we would have been for it at Khartoum. We sand-bagged all round the Fort and supplied men for the big gun teams and took up our various positions for the defence of Khartoum. Our Platoon's job was to defend the Water-Works. Luckily, however, the people of Egypt and the Sudan turned up trumps and would not sympathise with Turkey in her uncalled for declaration of war. At the proclamation of the new Sultan, all the Native Chiefs came from all over the Sudan to Khartoum and expressed to the Sirdar their loyalty to Britain. This, of course, removed all doubt and eased everybody's anxiety, the Sirdar's in particular. There are only about 400 of us here and I fear that we could not have held Khartoum for long. Things are now as quiet as can be and we are having a holiday every Wednesday. They put Defaulters on Guard now as we kicked against being put on last week.

I hope you have thanked Gertie Holmes on my behalf for taking so much trouble over knitting that woollen helmet. It's very kind of her altho' it is rather too hot for anything but [?] blouses and shorts out here. A good dress out here would be a pair of bathing-drawers from the Baths. There is a Race Meeting on to-day which starts at 3-45. Our Major is running his horse in one of the Events and as it is the first bit of excitement we've had for some time, I think I'll go. The Major told us this morning that we mustn't plunge heavily on his horse, as he didn't fancy it much. Fancy the irony of it! I don't think we could have raised 10/- in the whole Platoon, so it's not likely any of us will lose any money. I'm chucking it now and getting ready. So ta ta until to-morrow the Soldier's half-day. "Sa'eeda" which is Arabic for "Good-day" or "Salaam" which means "Peace be with you."

(Wednesday morning. Re-enter "Hearth-rug" in his déshabillé ie one shirt and one pair of shorts). To-day is the Soldier's holiday as I've said before. Reveille sounded at 6-30 and I didn't rise till 7 o'clock. I've never been in bed so late for over seven months and I had a fearful headache with staying in bed two hours overtime. However, I had a bath which washed it away. When I get home there will be great difficulty in keeping me in bed after 5 o'clock in the morning - perhaps. It's marvellous what one can get used to, isn't it? Whoever would have thought that your humble could have risen at 5 o'clock every morning without a murmur? Sometimes when we have something special on we get up at 4 am and 4-30. Unearthly, aint it? Next season, we'll arrange to get up early and play Tennis, shall us? By the way, I hope you'll be as adroit as of yore at Tennis, as I expect I will require some lessons to get me back into my renowned skill with the 'Pills'. I must also see if I can pick up a bit of your prowess in counting. I learned to my sorrow whilst playing against you last time that games can be lost and won by skill in counting and a vivid imagination. At deliberate bad memory I think you take the biscuit. Once, when I thought it was "Forty-fifteen" in my favour, I remember, you had the blooming impudence to claim the game. However, let's hope that I'll be able to hold my own against you a little better, when I get home. A little while back I bought a fine Racquet off one of the niggers for 7 piastres. It belonged to one of the Officers and there was a crack in it. I used it for a time and then suspected that it would not hold out much longer. Accordingly I sold it to a Sergeant for 20 piastres and, sad to say, it broke into two pieces a few weeks afterwards. It seems I had sold it in the nick of time.

The time does go slowly when there are no Parades. Most of our blokes are at present playing cards or else having a nap. The others are writing. At all events Wednesday can be utilised in pen-pushing. Ernie Shaw has resorted to Postcards now instead of letters. I intend to "stick it" with the letters if it kills me.

By the way, I'll be glad to hear that the two full-plate Photos have reached 91per the Boy Scouts. In all they cost me 5/10d in English which is a heap of brass for a Soldier. I've not paid for them yet but will do on Friday out of the 14/- Khedive Pay or Colonial Pay as it is now called since the Khedive got the bullet. It's quite a God-send! You might say that we only get 34 pence a week as a piastre (which is 2½d) only goes as far as 1d in England. A penny tin of blacking costs 2 p.t. and a pound tin of jam is 6 p.t. which is 1s/3d. I don't know, but I should think that you could get a pound pot of any kind of jam for 6d in England. Is that so? The other day we bought a tin of brawn. On opening the tin we had not much difficulty in getting it out. It poured out like soup. What I'd like more than anything would be some brown bread and butter. Some of Jane's home made brown bread preferred.

There is no Mail again to-morrow so we must wait till Sunday for letters. I have just had another squint through your letter. You seem to have got tied up in one or two places. For instance, you said that you tried to get <u>Ernie</u> at George's place at 5/- per week. Either you mean <u>Ridley</u> or else the sum you name must be £5 weekly. I think that Ridley really ought to have a better job than butchering, however acceptable the "backsheesh" joints might be. You will be again in your Glory romping poor Ridley round all the commercial houses in town. I tremble for Rid if you, by any chance, have any more shoes which pinch your feet. At all hazards, I sincerely hope they haven't patent leather toes. Fortunately, I think Rid is immune from danger as his feet, if I remember aright are of the policeman standard. It also behoves young Harold to cultivate fair sized understandings or else he, poor lad, will be another victim of feminine footgear. Your low shoes and a certain pair of clogs have played an important part in my career. When I think of the clogs, I can almost hear the fearful clatter down our entry at 108* when I came running home from school. Isn't it strange. A lad can go to school in any kind of old boots several sizes too big for him, but let him go in a good pair of clogs and his life will be made miserable. Perhaps the stealthy tread of a bloke on his uppers arouses no suspicion but the merry ring of a pair of clogs excites attention and brings everlasting disgrace on the wearer. To go to school in a pair of your father's old boots is allowed but in a pair of clogs! It's unthinkable, and mustn't be attempted in a school assembly like that of Upper Jackson Street School.

I'm sorry to hear of Tommy's unseemly behaviour. He must have some secret sorrow in his heart. Perhaps Saul's cat and others are throwing it in his teeth for not enlisting. Poor Tommy must be leading a dog's life. Maybe some cat or other has sent him a white feather. Our staff of animals has been reduced to two monkeys, the dog having left home and the goat and hyena disposed of. Every night the goat and hyena used to kick up a deuce of a noise and as we cannot lose our sleep, somebody took them both out and managed to lose them. We have a small monkey and a big one. The young 'un teases the life out of the old 'un and gets many a good hiding for its trouble. Monkeys are the most lively animals in the world. At home you don't see them to advantage as it is too cold for them there.

I wouldn't waste your money on a Fountain Pen if I were you. Thanks all the same. You can, however, slip one or two pen-nibs in with your next letter if you have any handy. This one I'm writing with is a brute.

I would like to hear all news of Teddy. I've not heard anything of him for a long time and hope he is alright. I hope he gets a furlough. If anybody deserves one, Teddy does.

Doug Sproat is a proper hero, isn't he? I'll bet he is in no great hurry to get back. What's-her-name used to turn up her nose at Doug being in the Liverpool Scottish at one now, didn't she? I suppose she has changed her tune now, eh?

I am so sorry to hear that John Green gets no better. You might remember me to him when you go round.

I'm about cleaned out now so with your permission will chuck it. Stan Newbould has had a week in Hospital. He only just escaped Appendicitis. However he is now alright. He has grown very fat. Ernie Shaw has put on a lot of weight. Talk about a "corporation." It's a bad thing to get fat out here. After a bit of skirmishing, Newbould comes off Parade like a wet-rag thoroughly worn out. I'm still like a whippet although I have put about 4 lbs on but it isn't fat.

At Khartoum we seem to be neglected in regard to issues of shirts etc. Most of us are sadly in need of socks, shirts, towels etc., but we cannot get them. The Quartermaster has ordered them repeatedly but they don't come. We all have ragged shirts of every variety of shirting. We should all have at least three grey-back shirts. These are fine shirts, being very thick and very necessary out here for keeping the sun off your back. You can get a touch of "sun" with wearing thin shirts. Thick woollen shirts are also preferable as they absorb the perspiration. A Regiment looks fine all dressed in blue greybacks, shorts and puttees but ours looks a rag and bobtail lot in all kinds of shirts. The Quartermaster is every day expecting them coming up but perhaps they have forgotten that there are any troops in Khartoum. . The blokes in Cairo and Alexandria get the pick of all the stuff and we get the hump. Our Camel Corps is still out on trek.

We are out at 4 o'clock in the morning on Field operations. Sand operations I should say. We had an idea that we had knocked off training but evidently it is not so. There are two "Waggers" attached to each Platoon and we are to get into communication with our Major. He has 4 "Waggers" and they communicate between the Colonel and us. We learn that visual signalling has been superseded by Field Telegraphy and Telephones at the Front but the Flags and Heliographs are very useful in an open country like this. Of course the Morse Code is always employed and we have a working knowledge of that now although we cannot go very fast yet.

I really must "stow it" now so I'll finish off. Again hoping that my Uncle and Auntie are quite themselves again and with heaps of love to everybody, I remain,

Your loving little brother
Matt   xxxxxxx

P.S. I've not had a letter from Jane or my Uncle for some weeks. Hoping for one soon. Tell Harold not to bother writing if he hasn't time. They had an Anthem at the Cathedral last Sunday. It was fierce! Some of the women sounded like cats.

P.P.S. I had nearly forgotten to send my love to Marie and all the girls in the office. Ta, ta.

* [Shrewsbury Street, Hulme]

Letter 22 - 5th April 1915

Khartoum, Sudan
Easter Monday 5th April, 1915

My dear big Sister,

A mail came in last Thursday and although some blokes got 6 and 7 letters, I got sweet nothing. However, last night I got your letter and a fine long one from Marny. My Auntie timed her letter nicely as I got it after coming home from Church. I am getting quite religious as I went to the Cathedral twice on Good Friday and also last night. I don't suppose there were many at Mr Price's place on Friday but they got a good crowd at the Cathedral. Last night the place was packed. There is really nothing else to do with our time now that football and all other sports have been stopped owing to the heat, and, consequently we look forward to going to Church on Sunday nights. Sunday is, without doubt, our best day as the Mail comes in on that day as a rule. After the service last night, the Choir gave a few items out of the 'Messiah'. One of our Officers, Capt. Smedley, sang "Darkness shall cover the Earth" and "The People that walked in Darkness" in fine style. I believe he performs in M/c Cathedral at home. A lady then sang "I know that my Redeemer Liveth" very nicely but she could have done better with a fresh pair of bellows. She was very short-winded and it cannot be wondered at in a place like Khartoum. The Choir then manfully struggled through "Even so in Life." I was hoping that they would have a shot at "Halleluiah" so that I could have a shout but the Choir, it seems, was too small to attempt it.

I say, kid, I didn't mean you to buy any recitations. I only wanted you to get the words written out, if you could. I hope this letter gets you before you have expended 1s/6d on "How we shaved the Barge." I thought that perhaps Georgie could let you have the words of one or two from his repertoire. I am returning the Photo of the Refuge would-be-soldiers. It's not a bad photo of me is it? I'm holding my nut on one side though, which won't do in the Army, will it? I don't think that one third of the blokes on that photo have been taken on. At least, they weren't at that time. Perhaps they are not so particular now in taking on Recruits.

I'm also returning the "Hinvite" to Sand's "do." From what you say, people can get in without a ticket if they take a good present. I can imagine Ma Sands standing at the door with her apron out. Let's see, it comes off tonight. Between me and you, I would rather be here in Khartoum to-night than at the King's Hall. That is saying a good deal for of all the places on this pimple of ours, preserve me from Khartoum. I can picture you reclining in the Buffet at the present moment. I wonder whether you will again be fortunate enough to collar the bit of custard to-night. Poor Mr Sands won't half get a "bashing" if he doesn't come up to scratch and do the honours. I wonder if she'll have the poor fellow jumping over chairs to show his obedience to Mrs Sands. And then there'll be poor little Norman got up like a Prize Rabbit and all the girls with shiny faces. On the quiet, this war has done me a good turn, as I have got out of the risk of being asked to two 21st birthdays at least, and what is of more importance, two Presents.

I say, kid, have you any use for Coral Beads? I can buy good sets for about 2s/6d or 12 piastres. If so let me know and I will be only too glad to get you a link. Perhaps I've mentioned it before. There is any amount of things to buy in the way of curios but, of course, a lot of the things are got up for selling to unsuspecting Tommies. Daggers made in B'ham, for instance!

Last week we had our fill of trench digging and we are at it again to-morrow from 6 to 9. From 5 to 8 to-morrow night we are bridge building. We erect tressle bridges from one bungalow to another. It is part of a soldier's training. A knowledge of ropes and knot-tying is also soldier's routine. I could do with my Da to give me a bit of tuition in the latter. From all accounts, what he doesn't know about ropes isn't worth knowing.

I nearly bursted when I read that bit of little Harold's about the name of [three words crossed out by the Censor] It's too funny for words.

The other day, one of the Cooks fried an egg in the sun on a piece of sheet- iron. If you put a piece of iron in the sun it gets red hot. Cairo is not a patch on this place for sun. They don't wear sun-helmets up there. They only have covers on their service caps. It's easily 20 degrees cooler than here out at Cairo at present. A bloke has just come back from Cairo and he says they were all wearing their serge during the day and greatcoats at night. It's a smelling place in some parts but there is plenty to see and amusements.

We'll all go "pots for rags" if we don't get some excitement shortly. There is a rumour current again that we'll get a move to France or the Dardanelles towards the end of May. I hope it's true. It would suit me down to the ground to be sent to the Dardanelles. We would then get credit for doing something. All stations are as good as one another in foreign parts in peacetime, but to be dumped here in war time is above a joke. I believe the Cheshires were only in India about two months before being sent to the Front. The East Lancs. Brigade (of which the 7th Manchesters form a Battalion) is supposed to lick the Cheshires hollow for efficiency and yet we're here.

There was a rumour that Frank Norbury and Ben Radcliffe have both been killed. It was true about poor Frank Norbury but not certain about Ben Radcliffe. I knew Frank Norbury well. He was a marvellous swimmer and I used to often play Water Polo with him in the Baths. I hope that the rumour about Ben Radcliffe is not true.

We have touched out for another Guard to-morrow night. We came off Palace Guard, Ernie and I, last Friday and sad to say, are on again on Wednesday, the soldier's holiday. They cannot find any Defaulters in the Battn to put on Guard on Wednesdays and so the Signallers have to take their turn. It's no use growling. I can do a Guard with anybody. It all passes time. The time doesn't half pass. We have been out in Khartoum over 6 months already and in the Army over 7 months. Getting old sweats, eh!

I am sending back Teddy's letter. He doesn't seem as cheerful as usual. Poor lad, he's had a rotten time during this last Winter and deserves a furlough. I must endeavour to drop him a line this week. I'm glad you are sending him Oxo cubes etc. I don't want anything. We are living in luxury compared with Teddy. We do get a proper bed even if the grub is not all that can be desired. It is chiefly bread and jam and soup, broken by tinned herrings or salmon, but personally, I'm not pawky in regard to grub. A lot of the blokes here kick up a row and throw the stuff about but I think that we are doing as well as it is possible in a place like this. It's so out of the way. We cannot get shirts for love nor money. We aren't half a ragged shirted lot. We are, indeed, having a "ripping" time with our shirts at all events. What's the use of growling. I'll swear that a lot of blokes, who are adept a[t] grumbling, are much better looked after here than they are at home. Yet they growl.

You'd be surprised at the ages of some of the blokes in the Sudanese Army. They all look young but some of the beggars are over 75 years of age. One of them, a Colour Sergeant, who works at the Palace is 85 years of age and is as straight and active as a chap of 30. He has over 50 years service in. It is the boast of the people of the Sudan that they possess the secret of perpetual youth. I think their food has a lot to do with it. The staple food is dhura and from this they make their bread, brew their beer and distil it into a kind of whiskey. There is a certain tribe, called the Dinkas, who live about 2 hundred miles up the White Nile from Khartoum. They are the tallest tribe in the world. Most of the women, and all the men are 6ft 6in and over in height. They are a cattle- rearing people. They live and die for the cattle, use cattle as money, and buy a wife with so many cows. Although averse to hard work, they will work three years for a cow. You see, they work for a cow, then buy a wife with the said cow and then are supported in idle luxury for the rest of their earthly career by the said wife. Looking at it from our point of view, a wife is hardly worth three years hard labour, is it? Although the fair damsel may not know, much less approve of, the young man, she has to marry him on the bloke paying over a cow or so to her dear father. It's a queer way of dealing with women but I don't think things will ever be altered, unless of course they start the Suffragette movement in the Sudan. It reminds one of "The Marriage Market" and that chap bawling out for every lot which was put up "Two cows!" Do you remember it? It's nearly "Lights Out" now so I'll chuck it till tomorrow. Ta ta. xxx

(Tuesday) I must chuck it now, as I must get ready for Guard tonight. This morning from 6 to 9 we had three hours solid trench digging. It nearly puts a bloke out. It's bad enough standing in the sun let alone digging and swinging a pick for 3 hours without a rest. We came back wet through and as usual had not a dry shirt to change into. The shirts are still coming. It's rotten knocking about all day in a wet, sweaty shirt.

This week-end, our Major has been paying a visit to the cotton plantations up the river. They grow some near Omdurman but it is only small stuff. It's very good quality, I understand. There is another Sentry coming out at the end of this month. The Editor, Major Hertz has gone home for three months for the good of his health and our Major, J. H. Staveacre has taken the job on.

I will conclude now till next week. Hope my Uncle is keeping better in health. Glad to hear that Marny is better. With heaps of love to Uncle, Auntie, your Harold and all the family at home and abroad. Also please do all that is necessary in regard to Tommy's progress down the steps. I shall be glad to hear all partics from Ted. Will write him now.

Heaps of love from
Your loving little brother
Matt
xxxxxxx

P.S. How do you like the paper? The blokes here want to know if I'm writing a book. They can't understand Ernie and I writing so much. Ta ta. Don't forget to keep up the correspondence. You deserve an Iron Cross already for pen- shoving.

Letter 23 - 9th April 1915

Khartoum

9th April 1915

My dear Uncle,

What ho! All is excitement here at Khartoum. This morning we heard officially that we leave Khartoum next Wednesday the 14th inst. Of course our destination is unknown. It's either the Dardanelles, France or India. We join our Division at Alexandria and move from there. I pity the poor blokes who are coming up to relieve us. We won't half give them a cheer. It will bowl a lot of them over, as the temperature is now 112 degrees in the shade. We are all confined to Barracks from 8 to 5 during the day and nobody can go out in the sun except on Guard. We had heard rumours for a few days but this morning the Orderly Officer said "Well judging by the noise, I suppose you've heard the rumour. Well, it's a fact. We leave Khartoum on Wednesday next certain." There wasn't half a roar. The blokes here are going dotty. We thought we had been forgotten. It's no' much notice, is it. Five days. However, we have been ready for a move for some time but nobody dared to hope it would come so soon. Our Colonel is too full for words and the Major in command of our Coy is as excited and eager as a hen with her first nest of chickens. The Colonel had all the Corporals and Sergts up this morning and said "Well, boys, our chance has come. We leave here on Wednesday. Pack your kit-bags and send all your curios home." The Adjutant then gave them a Lecture on "Billeting" which favours the opinion that we'll go to France. I hope so. Talk about medals after this lot! In addition to all the War medals, we'll get one for the annexation of the Sudan. The blokes here are kicking up an awful row.

I'm on Guard again to-night. Only came off last night. We'll be up to the neck in work now. We sleep on the desert for two nights, when the other blokes come. We don't mind how much work there is to do and there's no complaints about grub as long as we are on the move. There's an awful bustle on. We've got to pack up etc. Kit inspection. We are still without shirts but may get them at Alex. or Cairo. You may have heard of our move before this letter gets you. This may be my last letter for a while. Letters from you had better be addressed to the G.P.O. London. Don't forget to put 1/7th Man. Regt. and put East Lancs. Division on as well. Rest assured that I shall write on the first and every opportunity.

It's grand to think that we are getting out of this hole to do a bit of real soldiering. It's all one to us whether we shoot Germans or Turks. The boys who are relieving us must be in the Red Sea now. We won't half give them a welcome. We are all eager to know who they are. Must chuck it now as there are bags of Fatigues and heaps of work.

Give my luv to Marny and Cissie. Hope you are a lot better in health. Don't any of you get excited on my account. We'll pull through all right. With heaps of love to you all

> I remain (in haste)
> Your affectionate nephew
> Matt

Unidentified photo – possibly taken at Port Sudan.

Letter 24 - 13th April 1915

My dear Cissie,

This is our last day in Khartoum and between the many Fatigues and spells of hard work which are necessary on leaving a Barracks, I am trying to drop you a line. We leave early in the morning for Port Sudan. We embark there for Port Suez and train it to Cairo. We join the East Lancs. Div. at Cairo and then proceed to one of the theatres of War but whether it will be the Dardanelles or the Continent, nobody here knows. The Sirdar (who, I might remind you is our Hon. Colonel as well) reviewed us this morning, we marching past him in full pack in fine style and he then made his farewell speech. He was most warm in our praise and it did us good to listen to his appreciation of our services whilst at Khartoum. There was also a Presentation of Colours from the Egyptian and Sudanese Infantry Battalions at Khartoum. This honour has never been bestowed upon any other Regt. in the Sudan and naturally we are rather proud of it. We are the first Battn of Terriers to enter the Sudan and perhaps that accounts for the fuss they make of it. A lot of the Europeans in Khartoum stop us and tell us how sorry they are to lose us. We're not sorry to leave them, however. They say that our behaviour has been most gentlemanly.

I have not had a letter for a fortnight but perhaps there will be something waiting for us at Cairo.

They have sent a packing case with all the blokes' curios to Burlington St. We have to fire away everything except things which are necessary. I'd only a couple of links of coral beads to send, so I packed up all my correspondence and addressed the parcel to you. You'll see to it, won't you, kid. You might give one of the links of beads to a friend of mine, there's a dear, and shove the letters in a drawer like a sport, away from the madding crowd's ignoble gaze. We've all made our Wills out. I'll cut you off with a shilling if you don't stop reading my letters.

It's awful hard lines on the poor blokes who are coming to take our place. I've told you, perhaps, that they are the City of London Territorials (Royal Fusiliers) and I believe they have come from Malta. This place will crease the beggars. It's getting hellish and we are delighted to get out of it. A bloke from our Mess has just been carted to the Hospital with sun-stroke and there was one I helped to carry on the stretcher off Guard the other day with the same thing. 114 degrees in the shade is far from comfortable, I can tell you. I must chuck it now, kid.

I'm packed up and ready to move at a minute's notice. We've all got our ammunition in our pouches and are waiting for the train. There seems to be a firm opinion that we will come home but I don't see it myself. However don't be surprised to see us arriving at Plymouth. We may have to go up to Aldershot for training before doing any scrapping. Of course, nobody knows. My candid opinion is that we are for the Dardanelles. I'll bet Kaiser Bill and the Sultan of Turkey are in a terrible funk. Eh, what! I must chuck it now. So, hoping you'll do the necessary with the contents of the parcels, and with heaps of luv to Marny, my Uncle and everybody else,

I remain
Your loving brother
Matt

xxxxxxxxx

Matthew Richardson's will, as made out on the official form supplied to troops.

Short Form of Will
(See instruction 4 on page 1)

If a soldier on active service, or under orders for active service, wishes to make a short will, he may do so on the opposite page. It must be in his own handwriting and must be signed by him and dated. The full name and address of the person whom he desires to benefit, and the sum of money or the articles of property which he desires to leave to them, must be clearly stated.

The following is a specimen of such a will leaving all to one person:-

In the event of my death I give the whole of my property and effects to____

(Signature) JOHN SMITH
Private, No 1793
Gloucester Fusrs

Date

The following is a specimen of such a will leaving legacies to more than one person:-
In the event of my death I give £10 to_____
and I give £5 to_____
and I give the remaining part of my property to_____

(Signature) JOHN SMITH
Private, No 1793
Gloucester Fusrs

Date

WILL

In the event of my death I give the whole of my property and effects to my uncle Nicholas Ridley of 91 Cromwell Rd Stretford, near Manchester England.
Matthew Ridley Richardson
Private, No 2263
1/7th Manchester Regt.
9th April 1915

Letter 25 - 20th April 1915

S.S. Suevic
Port Sudan
20th April 1915

My dear Uncle

We are on board the "Suevic" waiting for the other half of the Battn coming up from Khartoum. The ship is in a filthy condition, the blokes not having cleaned it at all whilst they have been on board. The City of London Fusiliers are an awful mob not discipline[d], no Officers worth their salt and they are as dirty as pigs. Poor beggars, they've been bundled from Malta out here at an hour's notice. They got in an awful state at Malta and the ship was inches thick in dirt when they embarked a week ago. It is only a Cavalry Trooper and can accommodate 400 men and 500 horses. It's been bringing the Australian Cavalry from Sydney. There are over 800 of us to go aboard and <u>no</u> horses. Consequently 400 (me included) of our lot from Khartoum have a stall each. We are like horses. Of course there is bags of room but it isn't half "niffy." The blankets and hammocks are all 'merry' and we are having a lively time without doubt. Our Major refused to take the ship over at first and we had two days on the desert on bread and "bully." It's lively I can tell you but we don't mind so long as we are getting out of the Sudan. I've had 5 dips in the sea and it's grand.

The blokes who have been stationed at Port Sudan look fine and healthy. They don't half show us up. If we'd stayed at Khartoum much longer, we would all have "kicked the pail" I'm sure. We [are] all for Alex. first. Our second half comes up at 3 o'clock and we set sail to-morrow morning. From all accounts it's a steady boat. Of course it has to be for horses. We are getting some fine butter on board. First I've tasted for 7 months. This pen is a brute. I believe we are for the Dardanelles.

We don't half pity the Cockneys going up to Khartoum. They half [have] rotten N.C.O.'s and Officers and it must be heartbreaking for them to be shown up like we have done. They wouldn't believe we are only "Terriers." They have all joined since August and so you can imagine what their Officers must be like. They are all supposed to be trained but they look like a lot of sheep. The Sirdar will go mad when he sees them.

We got a bumping reception at Khartoum station when we entrained. All the ladies bought us tins of cake, and other luxuries. Must have cost them quids. All shaking hands etc. Awfully sorry to lose us. Of course they made such a fuss with us being "Terriers" but there is no doubt we have come on and I'll back our mob against anybody.

Must chuck it now. I've touched out for Orderly man on board again but I can do it alright. Anything to get away. These new blokes thought it hot at Malta at 85 degrees in the shade. At Khartoum it was 112 degrees when we came away. It nearly creased us in full pack. God help them. Heaps of luv to Marny Cissie and all in England. Have written Teddy.

> In haste, I remain
> Your loving nephew
> Matt

Unidentified photo from Matt's collection – lifeboat drill, possibly on board the SS Suevic.

Letter 26 - 26th April 1915

1/7th Manchester Regt
Abbassia Camp
Abbassia
Cairo
26/4/1915

My dearest Cissie

Well we are now under canvas and its rotten after Barrack life. There are only 24 in our tent and everything is upside down. We had a 26 hour train journey to Port Sudan, three days there on biscuits and bully beef, then embarked on the S.S. Suevic for Port Suez. Although we were on a horse boat we spent the best three days since leaving England on board. The crew were simply splendid and gave us everything possible in the "grub line." Four of us (E. Shaw included) bagged a whole chicken one night and soon put it out of action.

The Captain and Officers were greatly pleased with the way we set too and cleaned up the ship. The Fusiliers got the boat filthy. He (the Captain) said that we were soldiers but the Londoners were "scruff." Unfortunately good things (such as chickens for instance) don't last long and we had to disembark at Port Suez and entrain for Cairo. It was an eight-hour run and we got into Camp about midnight.

In coming up to Cairo we have "jumped out of the frying pan into the fire." It isn't half so hot but we are getting a working out. To-morrow night we are going on a full pack march 13 miles out. It will crease us as Khartoum has made us as weak as kittens. We cannot carry full pack very far. Coming from Khartoum we were carrying on an average 112 lbs per man. At times you feel as if you could aim kit bag, equipment, pack and rifle across the desert. I would take 2d for the lot. We are now "pigging it" under canvas but I don't think we'll be here above three weeks. I went into Cairo last night. It's an awful place. It was Sunday night and you never heard such a hullabalu in all your life. Cairo is supposed to be the worst place in the world and it's to be hoped it is. I'm blooming glad there are no such places in England. Old Cairo has been wiped out for some time now and new Cairo ought to be burned and a good deal of the people in it. Immoral isn't the word for it. We intend visiting the Sphinx and Pyramids next week when we get some "hoof." We are encamped next the Australians. There are 500 or so left in a convalescent camp. They are a fine big set of fellows but rotten to the core. No discipline nor any regard for anything or anybody. Must chuck it now. No facilities for writing, washing or anything. With heaps of love to everybody, Auntie, Uncle, Harold and all at home

I must conclude
In haste
Your loving brother
Matt   xxxxxx

P.S. Have just got letter containing the sample of your costume. You must look quite tricky. Wish I could take you to Church in it. Ta ta. The sooner we get out of this the better. Dardanelles it will be or else France. Not partic. which.

Unidentified photo from Matt's collection – the water is possibly the River Nile at Khartoum.

Letter 27 - 16th May 1915

Mediterranean Expeditionary Force
Sunday May 16th 1915

My dear Auntie,

After six days in the firing line we have come back to the rear dug-
outs and I hasten to let you know that I am quite well and in the
best of spirits. Whilst in the trenches I got a long letter from you and
as usual a long one from Cissie. It appears from Cissie's letter that
you are having a struggle with the household expenses and I think
that you ought to have mentioned it before and let me pay my share
towards the upkeep. Before relating our experiences in the trenches, I
must get this matter settled. Now there is 14/- (15/- I expect by now
as Jack Pieterson has had a 2/- advance) waiting at the Office to be
drawn every week. This is entirely at your disposal and you can have
the lot if you need it. I don't think Cissie will mind going round for
it and I am enclosing a note to Mr John Harrison which will perhaps
explain things. Cissie might also take this letter round as I'm sure Mr
Harrison will be pleased to know how we are faring and more than
pleased to let you have some brass without any fuss or inconvenience.
The money is due to me and I hope Cissie won't think that going for
it savours of going for poor relief. I wish you would have let me know
before that you were short and I could have easily allotted some of my
soldier's pay home. It is too late now however to do anything as we are
not drawing any pay in the field. Now I hope you will use as much of
the 15/- as you require. I hope that matter is now clear and will get
on with the excitement.

Our Battalion has been in action and come out in fine style. Our
casualties are only slight but we are not allowed to quote any figures.
The Turkish gunners are in a merry mood this morning and are

dropping shrapnel over our dugouts. It's poor stuff though and they don't do much damage.

[Five and a half lines have been crossed out by the Censor at this point and are unreadable]

Cannot write any more so must chuck it. Am in the best of health. Hoping you are the same.

Your loving nephew
Matt

Jane Ridley, or Marny, as Matt sometimes called his great aunt.

Letter 28 - 16th May 1915

Mediterranean Expeditionary Force
Sunday May 16th 1915

Dear Mr Harrison,

I regret that I have not been able to write you for some time but probably you will hear all there is to be heard from those who get letters. From a letter I have received from my sister it appears that they are having a struggle to make ends meet at home owing to the increased cost of everything through the War. I am writing to ask you if you will let my sister have my half salary or as much as they require. I don't know if it is necessary to give any written authority but am sending one in case it is.

From my letter home you will read of our Battalion's debut into the firing line and we have acquitted ourselves very satisfactorily.

[Four lines have been crossed out by the Censor at this point and are unreadable]

Pieterson, Newbould and I are in the pink of condition and we all wish to be remembered to all at the Office.

Hoping you will excuse scrawl as there is not much facilities for letter writing in a trench and trusting you will attend to this monetary matter for me.

I remain
Yours faithfully,
Matt. R. Richardson

Letter 29 - 22nd May 1915

Mediterranean Exped. Force
Sat. 22nd May 1915

My dear Cissie,

We are now in a Rest Camp near the Base. From the firing line we went into some Reserve Dug Outs for a rest i.e. digging communication trenches and the night before last we occupied some support trenches. It's all moving about from one place to another and wherever we go we always seem to be under shrapnel fire. It's much safer in the firing line and with plenty of grub and water I wouldn't mind being there altogether. I've said as much as I may now and perhaps you will hear more from the papers.

It's Whit-Sunday tomorrow somebody has just reminded us. This is a much nicer place than Pickmere. We had a little rain again this morning but it soon dried up and everything is quite dry again. We are all getting our backs up again after Khartoum. We get bags of grub and I'm always hungry. Cigarettes and tobacco galore. I've had three dips in the briny this last few days and may go for one after finishing this letter. I'm feeling A1 and if I get through without being punctured, I'll have had a good time. Spare bullets and shrapnel comes over the Camp night and evening and there is a rush for the Dug-outs. I hope you have a good Whitsuntide. Are you carrying the banner this year? Hope my Auntie and Uncle are well.

[A sentence has been deleted by the Censor at this point]

My last letter may have appeared shot-off. I wrote four pages but had to tear three up. Hard luck.

Must chuck it now. Stan. Newbould, Jack Pietersen and Ernie Shaw are in the pink. More than that I cannot say. Au revoir.

With heaps of luv to all
    I remain
        Your loving little brother
            Matt   xxxxxx

P.S. Don't think the Turks can last out much longer. Will be home not later than X'mas. Received the songs etc. Not much use here though. Also got the "Punch" from Marie, for which please give my hearty thanks. Have not, however, received a letter from her as yet. What about some of the Keatings or whatever it is you send Teddy? Ta ta.

Letter 30 (postcard) - 1st June 1915

Med. Exped. Force
June 1st 1915

My dear Uncle,

We've been in the trenches now for 8 days. Still in and feeling fit and well. Expect to come out shortly, when I will write letter. Don't worry yourselves by looking down casualty lists. They are very poor reading. Glad to say I'm not amongst the list yet. Buck up. Don't grin and bear it. Laugh and grow fat. Hoping you are are [all] well. Heaps of love to all at home.

Yours in haste

Matt

Letter 31 - 2nd June 1915

Mediterranean Expeditionary Force
June 2nd 1915
(Don't know what day it is.
There is a slight difference of opinion in our trench!)

My dear Cissie,

We are still in the trenches, where we have been for the last 9 days. There does not appear to be much prospect of getting relieved yet for a while so I am trying to get this letter through. I've been getting plenty of letters from you lately. The handkerchief and toothbrush came in the niche of time and you're a brick to keep on writing so often and sending things. The cotton shirts have not as yet come up but I'm sorry to say that I don't require them as my worldly possessions are quite heavy enough to hump about. All I want is some of the stuff you send Teddy for his companions (one box will do) and a clean nose rag at intervals.

I am feeling fine and large and as strong as a mule. Our Battn. has again been in action and suffered badly. [Last three words censored but just readable]. We advanced on three consecutive nights last week and you know what that means - loss of men, bags of digging in and no sleep for anybody. I won't go into any details and so you'll have no need to worry yourselves at home. We have done good work and got plenty of praise but we have had the price to pay. The fighting here is with picks and shovels and sandbags and the best navvies come out with least casualties. The Turkish snipers [last two words censored but readable] are the trouble. Whilst we are digging in or observing, they are potting at us and they don't often miss. They are armed with silent rifles with telescopic sights [the rest of this sentence has been censored]. Poor Stanley Newbould had his head blown off by a sniper the other day. We buried him at the back of the trench at night and next day I got the Chaplain to read the Funeral Service over his grave. Ted Harrison, I'm sorry to say, has been missing since the first day we went into the firing line three weeks ago. There is a remote possibility of his being taken prisoner but I think he is lying out in the open somewhere. We take careful notice of all the dead bodies we come across but have not seen him yet. I'll chuck it now as I can see you all worrying about me. Being our friends, I think it only right to let you know about them. We have been forbidden to discuss casualties in letters. Don't you bother about me. I'll be alright. I'm like a cat - got 9 lives and I'll be coming off the tiles some night before X'mas with Tommy.

I was sorry to hear of the rioting in M/c and breaking into people's shops whose only fault is that they have German names. Don't let's adopt German methods. The more I read of German outrages, the more I am convinced that we will succeed in this great conflict if we put up a good clean straightforward fight. Our cause is just and right must prevail. If it doesn't then the world won't be worth living in and it will be better if we all die fighting now. I hope no able bodied men took part in the brick slinging etc. They ought to join the Army and strike a blow at the real enemy and not these poor shop-keepers. I've volunteered for bomb and hand grenade throwing and went down to Headquarters this morning for practice. There are still a lot of openings for good brick slingers. We are very near the [word censored] trenches now. I'll not forget this Whit week in a hurry. We were at it night and day. Must chuck it now as we are only allowed one sheet. Buck Marny up a bit kid. Tell her we're not half dead yet. Pleased to see Italy has started. Heaps of love to Uncle, Auntie, your bit of trousers and all at home and in Stretford.

> I remain
> Your loving little brother
> Matt   xxxxxx

Letter 32 (postcard) - 4th June 1915

Mediterranean Exped. Force
June 4th 1915

My dear Uncle

Still in firing line and feeling in fine fettle. This is our 11th day and we are going to swipe the Turks over the hill before we go back to the Base. Hope we all do well. We are making the hill a birthday present to King George. No more now. Keep your peckers up at home and we will keep ours up. Love to all from

Your loving nephew
Matt

Letter 33 (postcard) - 7th June 1915

Mediterranean Exped. Force
The Base
June 7th 1915

Dear Uncle,

After 14 days in the firing line I have stopped a bullet. It's in the head over the eye. Most lucky squeek'e. Same bullet killed another chap stone dead. Am quite all right and only sorry that I am not with my Regiment as we have just done some splendid work. Lost all but 120 men though!

Your loving nephew
Matt.

Letter 34 - 9th June 1915

On board S.S. "Southland" ex "Vaterland"
Hospital Ship
9/6/1915

Dear Everybody,

As you will see I am on board a Hospital ship bound for either Alex. or Malta. I was wounded two days ago at midnight. I had written 2 Postcards but was unable to post them. Am sending them for what they may be worth. My wound is one of the most fortunate on earth. The bullet hit me just above the left eye and took the corner off without touching the brain. It's a rather dirty wound on account of me not having washed for so long. I've had it dressed three times and that seems to cause the pain. The old dressing sticks to my eyebrow and the wound and takes a lot of dragging off. The poor chap who got the bullet after me dropped dead without a sound.

There are 2000 cases on board and there are some pitiable sights. Eighteen poor chaps have died since we got on board two days ago. I was awfully vexed at being hit as we were to have been relieved 4 hours after. Our Battn. had 15 days of it, made three advances and then charged and took the Turkish first line. Only 120 men and 3 Officers were left though! It's rather hard luck on me after going through all that, to be put out just on time, isn't it? On the other hand I ought to thank God I wasn't put out altogether.

I don't know where I'll be able to post this letter but will have it ready to post when an opportunity occurs. I won't be sorry to land somewhere where I can get a wash and a change of gear. I have nothing but my suit, boots and socks and a shirt. Not even a hat nor a red cent and there is nothing on board. I downed my pack when we charged and reached the Turkish trench without grub or water but plenty of ammunition. I wish you could have seen us charge. We rushed about

250 yards. When we got to within 30 yards, the Turks left their trench (those who could) and we got down and picked them off with our rifles. Before we charged, our Artillery entertained them for two hours and played the deuce with them. Those who were left in the Turkish trench were fearful sights - simply covered with wounds. I put three or four out of their misery. I should expect the same doing for me if ever I got mutilated half as much as they were. We didn't take any prisoners. None are being taken on their side. The devils torture our chaps who are unfortunate enough to get into their hands. They are a treacherous lot and are composed of all sorts and sizes of men - Turks, Armenians, Greeks, Germans, blacks - in fact, a more mixed-up crew you couldn't conceive. I don't think this letter will be censored so I am going ahead without restraint.

I have made a few shorthand notes in my diary each day since landing on the Gallipoli Peninsula and they may be of interest when I get back. Our first spell in the firing line was merely a matter of holding. We had about 6 days and each night we were attacked. It was the most forward position in the whole line and had to be held until the whole line came up to it. Our "B" Coy made an unnecessary Charge one day, which lost some men for nothing. Our Platoon got in the wrong trench the first night and had to stay there all next day. At night we reinforced the firing line over the open. Rockets and star shells gave us away and the Turks turned their machine guns on us and scattered us all over the place. About half of us got into the firing line, where things were pretty bad. The Turks made 4 assaults that night and got to about 20 yards off our trench in the last venture. They were shouting "Allah!" and we were giving them lead. As is always the case they turned tail after getting half way and went back - those who could. I think they must be driven to these charges by the German Officers as they seem to come in such a half-hearted way. When we charged the other day we went mad and kicked up a hell of a row. They say that the Officers send them out and cover them with the machine guns. The Turks are in a fearful plight and were it not for their German Officers, I think they would throw their hands in. They are told that they will only be shot if they surrender. In the second bout in the firing line, we made 3 advances to straighten the line and then on the 4th June (Friday) after two hours bombardment the whole line charged. On the right however, the Frenchies retired and then the Marines also retired. Then came the M/c Brigade. We were the right of the M/c Brigade but we held on. On our right Turks were in the same trench. I was bombing them and sniping them for 2 days. I was the only one left of our bomb throwers. During the two days after the Charge I shot 8 Turks at 15 yards range through a loophole along our trench. I also had a rifle trained at 300 yards on their trench. It was infilade fire and I bagged at least 10. It was just like rabbit shooting but they got me at the finish. The Officer nearly went mad as I was bringing them down. I never bothered about eating or sleeping with the excitement but I could hold my rifle as steady as a rock. Had I stuck it and got back to the Base without being hit, I've no doubt the Officer would have recommended me for a DCM or something. As it is I suppose I'm out of it. Perhaps well out of it.

There are too many of us on board to get looked after properly. There are hundreds hit in the hands and arms and not many head wounds. It's usually all over if you get it in the head. At our table last night out of 10 of us, 6 had to have their bread cut and buttered. About half the wounds are in the legs. They can't get down to the grub and the others when the[y] get down, can't grab it on account of the wounded arms and hands. I can get down to it and grab with the best of them but it hurts me to eat. I'm as hungry as a hunter. I had practically nothing for 3 days and when I came on board I went ravenous. Oh! for a bath and a change of togs. I suppose we'll get all that when we get in Hospital.

There is no need for any of you to worry as I expect I shall be all right again in a few weeks. Talk about one-eyed Gunner! I've got a bandage over my eye and all round my head. They put the Field dressing over both my eyes and told me to get to the Base if I could. It took me 3½ hours to get to the Dressing station, where they did me up, put me on a cart (where I fell asleep) and I was on board a tug at 9 o'clock. We reached Limnos and got aboard the Hospital Ship at 7 o'clock. I slept on deck all night in the cold and next day we got a bunk each. I'm not half giving it "bunk." We stood at Limnos a day and are now on full steam for either Alex., Malta or England. Must chuck it now. Heaps of love to all. Don't get excited. I'm quite alright. Hope you are all well. Now then Marny don't get alarmed. Ta ta.

Yours with a bandage on
Matt   xxxxx

Letter 35 - 11th June 1915

Geziah Palace Hospital
Cairo 11th June 1915

My dear Cissie,

I've struck "ile" and am living in the lap of luxury now. We disembarked at Alex. and boarded a magnificent Hospital Train for Cairo. Motors met us at the Station and brought us down to here. This place used to be the abode of some big Pasha who kept 600 wives and it's a grand place. Bags of fine grub and nurses and spring beds. Oh it was fine to get a bath and get into clean pyjamas. I'd not had my old trousers off for about 8 weeks and they weren't half "merry." We've fired off everything and they are being fumigated and washed. Mine could have done with burning.

I can't get to sleep at nights yet as it is too comfortable. It is a big change after sleeping in a trench with just your greatcoat on. I've lost all my gear in the Charge but will no doubt get rigged out again before being sent back. I don't expect I shall be here very long as my wound is doing "top hole." We get every comfort here but I won't be sorry to get back to the lads again. I want to finish for good and get home. I find it a big change after roughing it so long. I feel quite shy when the nurses speak to me. "I'm shy Mary Ellen, I'm shy". Mine's a clean lucky wound with no complications and no anxiety so don't any of you worry. Hope you are all well. Heaps [of] love to everybody. Don't let Marny get excited. Must chuck it now.

Your poor wounded war-worn Tommy
Matt. xxxxxxxx

P.S. Don't know how I'll go on for letters. Hope you ain't sent any parcels. Cheers!

Letter 36 - 15th June 1915

From Pte Richardson M. R. 1/7th Batt. Man Regt A Coy.
Ghezireh Palace Hospital
Cairo
(Spelt differently that's all. Same place)
15/6/1915

My dear Uncle,

The postman will be wearing his boots out over me if I continue writing so often whilst I'm in "dock": [Six words censored] but I don't want to be here long. I'll perhaps get sent to a Rest Camp in a week or two. Hope it's up at Alexandria. There'll be a bit of bathing there. It's getting very hot here in Cairo now and I've gone as weak as a kitten. I felt as strong as a horse up in Gallipoli Peninsula. The hill we were operating against was (and still is) called Achi Baba (Archie Barber we call it). I hope they hurry up and take it. There were thousands of troops waiting to be landed as we came away on the trawler. They should have been at least three days earlier in landing. As I've said in previous letters, we were open on the right flank through the Frenchies and Naval Brigade retiring. We were the Right of the M/c Brigade and this accounted for us losing so heavily. You see, the Turks all came back to their positions and were bombing and getting infilade fire on us. Of course we were busy at them and they must have suffered enormous losses. Our Artillery gave them soaks [?]. Another bloke and I hoisted an Artillery shield at the extreme right of our trench to show how far we occupied it. It was a red cloth arrangement and was riddled with bullets as we put it up. The other chap got hit and I had to get it up as best I could. The Artillery saw it immediately and opened fire straight away. By Jove! They did give it them hot. Shrapnel was bursting right in the trench where the Turks were and all the way up a Ravine where their reinforcements were coming up. Those French 75 cm and 4.7

guns were doing all the damage. The French Artillery is splendid.

It was funny at sunset and dawn to hear all the Turks chanting their prayers. Our lads used to set up in opposition.. One night crowds of them came running to our trench shouting "Manchesters, very good. Turks no want to fight." We'd been gulled before so the order came "Rapid fire" and they didn't stay long. Things have got to such a pass out there that we have had to abandon all rules of War. They have repeatedly made improper use of the White Flag, and when given an Armistice on one occasion to bury their dead, the blighters started digging themselves in and consolidating their position. They also shell the Base Hospital and Dressing Station daily so you see things have got into a rotten state. I am confident that hundreds of the Turks would give themselves up only they are afraid of being shot down as they come in. Of course, their German Officers encourage this opinion amongst them and they are literally "between the Devil and the Deep Sea." Must chuck it now. Hope you are all well at home. Wish it was all over and I was home again. I had 5 weeks out on the Peninsula and it was quite long enough. For all that I was "narked" at being shot and I shall be glad to be amongst the lads again - what is left of them. All the Regiments have suffered in the 29th Division. They knew the cost before we charged. Heaps of luv to you all at home.

I remain
Your loving Nephew
Matt.

Letter 37 - 16th June 1915

From Pte. Richardson M.R.
1/7th Batt Man Regt "A" Coy.
Ghezireh Palace Hospital
Cairo
(Same place only this time I have spelt it correctly)
16/6/15

My dear Uncle,

I have just been before the Medical Board and I think I'm coming home. They said I wouldn't be fit for over two months and I've heard from the Sister that all those cases are going home. I think it must be on account of the heat in Cairo. It is getting unbearable. Of course I don't know anything for certain, but I hope it is so. Will let you know definately, when I get to know definately.

18/6/1915

Wounds won't heal here on account of the heat and all cases that can be moved are being sent home. I will let you know when we are coming.

I read a fine account of the fighting and operations in the Dardanelles in "Land & Water" of May 8th 1915. The article is by Hilaire Belloc with three maps and although a good deal of the information as to the operations is to a certain extent anticipated, it has turned out correct. If you want a detailed account of our work in the Gallipoli Peninsula, I should recommend you to buy this paper. It's a weekly journal and the price although 6d, is worth it for the information as to our Allies and our movements in the different theatres of War. When I get back I can explain matters by the aid of those charts. I have taken rather a deep interest in our doings on the Peninsula - rather deeper than most Private Tommies I think. Most of the reports you get in the daily newspapers are "bosh" and this is the only account, which I have seen to be at all reliable. To read some of the accounts, they would have you believe that we are in occupation of the whole peninsula. When I left we were at the base of Atchi Baba the first hill, which is about 750 feet high. We are right up against their main line of defence, which is at the bottom of the hill. The slopes of the hill are free from trenches and I think we'll have to go round it. The idea in taking Atchi Baba is to mount big guns on it and so get a sweep all along the Peninsula. The New Zelanders and Australian troops are operating from Gaba Tebe against the Turkish right flank. They are at present waiting for us to advance as being so small a body they couldn't hope to successfully cut the Turks off from the rear. When I left, things badly needed fixing up and the line straightening again. This I believe has been accomplished and the whole line has come up level. I'm writing all this not knowing whether it will all be blotted out by the Censor.

A String Orchestra came to give us a tune yesterday afternoon and it was fine. There were 6 violins and it sounded grand. We used to get a bit of music from our Brass Band at Khartoum but I don't think it's in the same street as the String Bands. They also brought cigarettes with them and you may guess they got a good reception. I must chuck it now. Hope you are all well at home. I expect to see you soon. The sooner the quicker.

With heaps of love
I remain
Your loving nephew
Matt.

Letter 38 - 21st June 1915

From Pte. Richardson
1/7th Batt Man Regt. 'A' Coy.
Ghezireh Palace Hospital
Cairo
21/6/1915

My dear Cissie,

There's a Mail goes to-day so I am just dropping you a line. It's awfully "dosey" in Hospital - nothing to do but sleep, eat, smoke cigarettes and read occasionally. A little writing is quite a change. You cannot grumble about not having letters since I've been in dock, can you? Not about quantity at all events. The quality, I'll admit, is a bit rotten and not a bit like the type-written epistle which you sent from one of your picnicing boys. His was an innovation in soldier's letters, wasn't it? The typical Tommy's letter is "Just a line to let you know I am going on alright. Many thanks for the tobacco and fag-papers." Talking about cigarettes, our blokes were desperate in the firing line for smokes. Personally, I don't rave about smoking but when there is an issue of cigs, I smoke them. However, we didn't get many down there and a lot of the blokes would rather have been short of rations than tobacco. I've seen chaps cut a bit of dirty thick twist up and make a cigarette out of a letter from home - sometimes an old envelope. No sooner has the chap got the cigarette well alight, then about five or six others apply for the end of the fag. Thick twist doesn't make nice cigarettes but they seem to enjoy it when they can get nothing else. They don't crave for beer. I suppose they must forget that there is such a commodity. The majority of the tobacco and cigarettes intended for the firing line, never gets there. The last issue I got before coming away was one cigarette per man. I did rather well for smokes however as we used to light bombs with a cigarette. At night-time a match shows up too

116

much, so we used to get cigarettes off the Officers to light the bombs with. When we took the Turkish first line there was a bomb every two yards which should have been thrown at us. We collected them all and threw them at the Turks. Not bad is it - bombing them with their own bombs?

Well kid there's nothing doing yet in regard to sending me home. I'm afraid I shall be a fixture here for a bit, worse luck. It's rotten here in Cairo and getting hotter every day. It's a bad place for healing and I shall not be sorry to get out of it. I suppose everybody is looking blue in Lancashire. All the Lancashire Regiments have suffered heavily in the Dardanelles. Lancs always seems to drop in for the brunt of the fighting. Have you seen the full Casualty List for our Regiment? We have got it stiff. We were given a position of honour on the right flank of the M/c Brigade - the honour of getting cut up. Still somebody had to do it and we did what was asked of us. Must close now. Hope my Auntie and Uncle are quite well. I've not seen a letter for ages and there doesn't appear to be any prospect of getting one. There must be a bagful for me somewhere. Heaps of love to every body.

I remain
Your loving brother
Matt.   xxxxxx

P.S. Hope Teddy is alright. Hope he is still with the Royal Engineers. Ta ta

Letter 39 - 1st July 1915

From Pte. Richardson M. R.
1/7ᵗʰ Batt Man Regt. "A" Coy.
Citadel Convalescent Depôt
Citadel Barracks
Cairo

1/7/1915

My dear Cissie,

I have got another fresh home. I was discharged from Hospital yesterday and sent here to "convales." It's an awful hole - more like a prison or a workhouse than a Convalescent Home. It's simply alive with bugs and the grub is as rotten as they could possibly give us. I cannot stand it so this morning I asked the Doctor to send me back to my Regiment. He said he would send me out in a day or two. My head is still a bit sore but it will go alright. I suppose I'll be sent down to Alexandria and after getting a fresh rig-out, I'll get sent out with a draught for the Dardanelles. It's a beggar. In the Hospital they said I was for home. Perhaps they meant "Heaven." I don't object to roughing it in the trenches but I can't stand being eaten alive here when we are supposed to be recruiting our health. I didn't half get a mauling last night. Bug bites all over me. They weren't half pleased to meet me. This morning I took my bed to pieces and there were thousands of 'em in all the joints. Shrapnel and lyddite wouldn't shift the beggars so I painted all my bed with Creosote and killed thousands, in addition to taking many prisoners, and ammunition and machine guns.

It's been a big blow to us fellows coming from Ghezireh Palace Hospital. There we were living in marble halls and it's no joke coming down to whitewash. The bugs etc are extra. The way we get bossed and ordered about gets me down. It might be our fault that we got wounded. I'm getting out as soon as poss., sooner if necessary. I dare say I could hang on here for a month or two but it isn't in my line. I'd rather take my chance with another bullet than be treated like a pauper.

I've not had any letters yet. I trust and hope you are all well. Hope my Uncle and Auntie are in the pink. There must be a cartload of letters for me somewhere between here and Turkey.

I'll let you know, of course, when I am sent back to the Front. Won't be sorry to see all the lads again. I'm dying to know how things are going on out there. Must chuck it now. Heaps of love to all at home. Buck Marny up a bit. This can't last for ever, can it.

> Heaps of luv
> From your loving brother
> Matt.   xxxxxxxxxx

P.S. (later) Have just been told to pack up for Alexandria by 8.15 train to-morrow. What ho! Things are moving again at last. It won't be long before I'm Turkey shooting again. It's fine to be doing something again, ain't it? Have they booked you and Marny for shell-making yet? Be careful. They have a nasty trick of going off. Those I've seen have anyhow. Ta ta, old dear. xxxx

Letter 40 - 5th July 1915

Mediterranean Base Headquarters

42nd Division

Mustapha

Alexandria

5th July 1915

Dear Everybody,

As you will see I am at another place again. I am at the Base here at Mustapha awaiting to be sent out to the Dardanelles again. Almost the first thing I heard on arriving was that I had won the Distinguished Conduct Medal. I went to the Orderly Room yesterday and saw it in print - sanctioned by King Jud himself. I could have jumped for joy, as you may imagine. I suppose you at home will have heard before I myself knew about it. I'll bet my Auntie put her Sunday feather boa on immediately on hearing the good news.

Now I suppose you'll want to know full particulars of what it was for. I cannot tell for certain. It could have been for bomb throwing, sniping, brainy ideas or the following little adventure which I had - perhaps I suppose for the whole show combined. I've not mentioned this little episode before so here goes. On the morning after we took the first Turk trench, they tried to rush us and retake the trench. Well, from somewhere or other our chaps got the order to retire and they all got out and ran for it. I had a sort of affection for this trench we had charged and taken and I was wild at seeing all our blokes running away and deserting it. I was blazing away all the time at the Turks and shouting at the top of my voice - calling the Turks some awful names. The Sergeant Major was about the last to get out and he said to me "Come on Richardson, we've got to retire." I was mad and, firing all the time I said, "Well I ****** if I'm going to retire. I'd sooner be shot than run away from a lot of so and so Turks." All the time I was blazing away and getting my man with every shot. I'll bet I got off the regulation 15 rounds to the minute. Talk about rabbit shooting. They didn't half bowl over. When they charge they all bunch together and it is the easiest thing in the world to shoot them down. Well, the Sergeant Major came back after my forceable persuasion and we kept the beggars out. A few of them got to within 15 yards before we brought them down. I simply couldn't miss at that range and they all went back - those who could I mean. I am sorry to have to admit that I was swearing at the top of my voice - calling the Turks some awful names in my invitations to them to come on. However, we kept them out and so held the trench. I went and got reinforcements from another Battalion, and so we managed to hold on although it was touch and go, I can tell you. Of course I don't know whether this little incident was mentioned in my recommendation for the D.C.M. or whether I got it for bomb-throwing and sniping. You'd be surprised but although it was so exciting, I could hold my rifle as steady as could be and brought lots of Turks down, some at point blank range. If I'd have been firing my Course that day, I'll bet I would have passed out as "Marksman." It was the finest bit of sport I've had in my life although when I look back on it, I cannot help but wondering however I came through with only a flesh wound. I feel as proud as Lord Kitchener himself at having been awarded the medal and only hope that I pull thro' to have it presented. I can see my poor photo being in all the Picture Papers and admired by all the girls who read the pictures going down to town in the mornings. "What a noble face" I'll bet some of them say whereas if it was published for anything else, it would be "What an ugly looking beggar"! I'll bet you never thought you'd got a real live hero in the family, did you?

It is the first and only award out of our Battalion so far so I ought to be proud, oughtn't I? The little incident I've just told you doesn't reflect much credit on our Battalion so I should be glad if you'll keep it quiet. I've not said anything about it and, on second thoughts, can't think that it was mentioned in my recommendation - not the full particulars at all events. You could hardly blame them for retiring as we went through such a lot of bloodshed and trials, and the majority had lost their nerves. It was an awful ordeal and the trench was full of our chaps either dead or wounded.

Well, I'm still without any news from you. It upsets everything when you get wounded. I hope and trust everything is going well with you all. I'll, perhaps, be going back sometime this week. I have to pass the Doctor first. We are doing Fatigues here at the Base. I had about 3 weeks free-wheel, whilst in Hospital. I think I deserved a bit of a rest after ten months "grind" but they seem to be getting the blokes off again as soon as their wounds heal up. There are, of course, a lot of cold-footed old sweats hanging after jobs at the Base. They make you sick to see them.

I must chuck it now. Hope the Censor doesn't drop across this letter. He'll get eyestrain and serve him right. I hope Teddy is alright. It's awful not hearing anything from you but I suppose I will have to make the best of it. There must be a cartful of letters for me somewhere. They will no doubt be following me about from one place to another.

Well, I've done enough writing now I think. Excuse the bad writing and composition. Perhaps I'm too excited over the medal to write a good letter.

With heaps of love and kisses and other articles I must chuck it and conclude and remain

Your loving nephew
Matt.

P.S. I'm investing my last ½ piastre on a stamp to ensure that this letter won't be censored by any of our Officers. The Major in command of our Base was most profuse in his congratulations. Our Battalion, I hear, numbers somewhere about 250 and not 120 as at first we thought. About 170 were missing but I understand have since turned up. Ta ta.

Ernie Shaw was alive and kicking when I left on 7th June. I believe all the Battalion have had 2 weeks holiday at Hembros.*

* [The island of Imbros]

Letter 41 - 6th July 1915

Mediterranean Expeditionary Force
Alexandria
Egypt

6th July 1915

My dear Cissie,

Am going back to the Dardanelles first thing in the morning. Could have done with another week here but it was not to be. The bathing is fine. After 3 weeks in Hospital I got awfully soft and I could have got as hard as nails with about a week's bathing. Still one has the satisfaction of knowing that I'm not shirking my duty. I've got a new complete set of clobber, rifle etc. I've just been paid. Drew the enormous sum of 1/s. I'd about £4 owing on my Pay Book and they could only find it in their hearts to fork out a miserable 1/s. If I had my way I'd put all the Staff at the Base right up in the firing line, and bring our lads out for a rest. I suppose I oughtn't to grouse about pay at a critical time like this but soldiers live by grousing. They grouse most about trivial matters, but when called upon to rough it and lose their lives, there is not a murmur. Such is the nature of the beast - taken as a whole I mean. There are exceptions but they invariably get down and settle at the Base.

Well, kid, what do you think about your little brother's DCM? I'll bet all the Post Office Staff knew before you could say "Jack Johnson." You won't half be able to crow over those girls, whose brothers sent them such nice things from Egypt. I'm writing this in the dark kid so 'cuse bad scrawl won't yer?

I've not had any letters yet but will probably find a lot on landing in Gallipoli Penin. I sincerely hope you've not sent any parcels as if you have, they are sure to have been opened when I was found to be wounded in the head. They usually have not further use for parcels, when a bloke stops a bullet with his head. At least they don't think so out there.

Must chuck it now, kid. Hope and pray for the best. I must pull through without being killed, even if it's only to get my medal. I would give everything I had in the world - medal included - if it would bring this War one day nearer the end. It will be all over by X'mas. So roll on Xmas. Hope Marny and my Uncle are in the pink. Give my love to everybody, won't you? Must chuck it now, so ta ta for the time being. With heaps of love and kisses to you all.

I remain
Your loving brother
Pte M R Richardson DCM.
SWANK.

Letter 42 - 16th July 1915

My dear Uncle,

Still in the support trenches. We are doing well now and don't expect Turkey to last long. Shall be glad when they do throw in as it may be the beginning of the end of this terrible struggle. We heard the good news about Botha putting a stop to the Germans in East Africa. I hope the next good news will be Turkey's downfall.

I am still quite well and hope you are all keeping fit at home. You must all keep your peckers up and look on the bright side of things. My letters have gone sadly awry since I was wounded but perhaps I'll be getting them again now that I'm back with my Regiment. The Manchester Brigade has gone through it and had the lion's share out here and we every day hear rumours about our being sent home to be reorganised for France. We live on rumours.

How's the garden? Glad to hear you have been in better health lately and hope my Auntie is in the pink and not worrying over this War. Was glad to hear from Cissie's letter that Teddy is still alright. He is a marvel sticking it in France since the beginning of the War. Don't know how he does it. We're "fed up" with this lot out here and haven't been out five minutes compared to our Teddy. Still we never get any rest here and the Base and everywhere is under fire. When we are supposed to be having a rest from the firing line we are out digging every day. Still it can't last for ever, can it? Hope you'll write pretty often as it does cheer a bloke up. I get quite excited when the Mail comes and we all leave grub and everything to read letters.

Must chuck it now. It's too dark to write much more and I think I'll get down for the night. Give my love to Marny, Cissie and everybody at home.

With heaps of love
I remain
Your loving nephew
Matt

P.S. Don't send any parcels. I've not got the last one you sent. Ta ta

P.P.S. I believe we move up to the firing line to-day. There is another charge coming off. This hill has to go at all costs this month as the weather breaks up soon and this Peninsula is terrible in the winter. Ta ta. Hoping to pull through.

Letter 43 - 23rd July 1915

Mediterranean Expeditionary Force
G.P.O. London
23rd July 1915

My dear Cissie,

We are back again in the reserve trenches and things are very quiet indeed. To-day something must be moving as we are all to remain at our posts because of a heavy bombardment which is coming off. It is very hot here now and <u>flies</u> - they eat you alive. They bother us more than the Turks. There is not much to write about. Ernie, Jack and I are in the pink and doing bags of work. We get our rest in the firing line. When we are out, there are loads of Fatigues - navvying - light portering and dock-labouring and since I've been back, I've been on them all. The Sergeant has an idea that I'm strong after my month's spell in Hospital. I'm certainly fatter than I was but flabby. Our battalion looks about played out - war-worn isn't the word. I wish it was all over. Trench warfare ought to be abolished. It's not fighting. It's digging victories. After all the digging I've done, I'll be able to whip round our garden in no time when I get back. I still get no letters. They will in all probability be chasing me round. It's rotten. After the affair of June 4th our lot got a week's rest at Imbros, a Greek* island not far away.

How are you all getting on? I hope you are keeping cheerful and in good health. I'm feeling alright now. Have got hardened again. I only see Ernie Shaw occasionally now. He is on transport work and lives on the beach. I'd rather be in the trenches than messing about with mules. Have not received the parcel yet, kid. The Keatings does heavy damage and I'm looking forward to the Pomade. It's funny to see all the chaps with their pants off, inflicting heavy losses on the enemy. We get plenty of bathing when we are in the reserve line of trenches.

I'll have to take you to the Baths when I get home. Of course, I'm presuming that Mixed Bathing hasn't been stopped. I hope my Auntie is keeping cheery thro' all this trouble. It's not half so bad if you take it smiling.   I must chuck it now. Heaps of love to Marny, Uncle, Harold and everybody at home. I'm still of opinion that it will all be over by X'mas and am looking forward to going round with the Choir, howling. What wouldn't I give to drop in at Choir Practice next Thursday? With bags of love I must conclude now and remain

       Your loving Brother
       Matt xxxxxxxx

P.S. Have not had a letter from my Uncle for ages. Glad to hear he is keeping in good health. Hope Teddy is still alright. You might give me his regimental number next time as I've lost it along with all my belongings after the Charge. Ta ta. Luv. Matt.

*[Imbros is now Turkish]

Letter 44 - 28th July 1915

Mediterranean Expeditionary Force
G.P.O London
28th July 1915

My dear Uncle

I think it is your turn for a letter. I haven't had any letters for a long time but perhaps it will work right again in time and I will probably be getting a bagful one of these days. Things are very quiet here at present. I suppose it's a lull - before the storm. We seem to be waiting for each other to come on. One's frightened and the other daren't.

Jack Pieterson sprained his ankle yesterday and he has been sent to Limnos, I hear. He was badly in need of a rest. With Ernie Shaw on the Transport, all my pals are now gone but everybody is pally out here. I am at present knocking out with a chap called [?]Hammond. He has been wounded and came back just before me. He got a bullet through the back of his neck, and he was only away 18 days with it. He only went to Limnos and he got treated very badly. Still he's a very cheerful sort of chap and we get on very well together.

I was inoculated the other day against Cholera. I'm now proof against anything - Typhoid, Cholera, Small-pox and we have got gas helmets and respirators in case the Turks use gas. All we want now is to be inoculated bullet-proof. This is not a suitable place for gas or I think the Turks would have used it long ago. The winds are gusty and sweep across the Peninsula as a rule. At present we are in the last line of trenches and we are allowed to go bathing or on fatigues - more of the latter than the former. I take full advantage of the bathing and had two dips this morning. To see our chaps splashing about in the Dardanelles or in the Gulf of Saros, one wouldn't think there was a war on. I think I've done more bathing this year than in all my life before. Nearly all of us are alive and we have a good set-to at least once a day. And great is the slaughter thereof.

Hope Teddy is still alright. You don't say much about Ernie and Ridley. Hope Ernie won't enlist. Two out of one family is quite enough. If he is got to join anything, tell him to join the A.S.C. If I'd have joined the A.S.C. I'd have been a Sergeant Major by now. I saw a bloke from our place the other day. He's just come out here and he's nothing less than a Quartermaster. I wouldn't exchange him jobs at the Office but he's got a fine job out here.

Must stop now. Hope my Auntie and Cissie are in good health and spirits. This War will end as abruptly as it began and not later than X'mas. With heaps of love to all.

I remain

Your loving nephew

Matt

P.S. I'm in the pink. Hope you are keeping well. Ta - ta

Letter 45 - 1st August 1915

British Mediterranean Expeditionary Force
Sunday August 1st 1915

My dear Cissie,

I had a windfall yesterday and received your parcel and some rather ancient letters. The box was in pieces but I'm glad to say nothing was lost or wasted. Everything was most welcome and you're a brick to go to such trouble and expense. I am now well supplied with Insecticide and the little devils are in for a hot time. I couldn't read Teddy's letters for chocolate but I gather that he is still alright. Your letter enclosed in the parcel was dated 29th May and I also got one dated 7th June. I got a letter from Albert Shaw and also one from Marie Worsley so you see I got quite a treat yesterday. Reading letters with a mouthful of chocolate is about the height of luxury.

At present 25 of us are in a Redoubt and I'm endeavouring to write at least 4 letters between reliefs from "watch". This Redoubt is rather a decent place, as strong as a castle and personally I could stick it for the duration. I hear though that we go in the firing line tonight. I've been back nearly a month now and am feeling fine. I think Jack has gone to Limnos with his ankle. I saw Ernie Shaw the other day and he is not so grand. He's got diarrhoea again and it does pull a bloke down. I had a ride on his old moke or horse. It's hard to say which it is. It's got two speeds - slow and stop. Although Ernie does not get in the trenches, he has bags of work to do especially when our Battalion is going in again after a rest. "Rest" I said. W. o. r. k. - "Rest." Of course, Transport men don't do bayonet charges and that goes a long way with some people. There's not much news this time. There's not much doing. Just a little fireworks at night time - evening [?] hate.

Have not heard from Marny or my Uncle for ages. Get them to drop me a line. Hope they are not worrying themselves unnecessarily.

Sorry to hear about Mother being ill. Hope she is better by now. I suppose you'll be driving a "hansom" or making shells ere this in your spare time. Don't think you'll get much spare time though with two brothers to write and send parcels to. Must close now. Hope everything is going on alright at home. Give my love to Auntie, Uncle, your bit of trousers and them all at home, won't you.

With heaps of love and kisses
I remain
Your loving brother
Matt xxxxxxxxx

P.S. Teddy is very optimistic, isn't he? Don't know how he manages it, do you? It's August Bank holiday to-morrow. I think I'll borrow Harold's "gigger" and go to Pickmere. Are you coming? I suppose you'll be all "Service" eh? No wonder the grass doesn't grow when George used such violent language when he misses the ball. You should warn him off the turf.

Letter 46 - 6th August 1915

C/o G.P.O. London
6th August 1915

My dear Uncle,

We came out of the firing line last night into the support line. I went for a dip this morning and now feel as fit as can be. Twenty five of us were holding a Redoubt for 4 days and we had 4 days in the firing line. We expect to be in these support trenches for another 4 days. I could do with it better if we got a decent rest after being in the line. Last night we hadn't been out of the firing line three hours before I and nearly all the Platoon were nailed for carrying ammunition up to the line. The only possible chance of getting a rest out here is by stopping a bullet. Of course, the difficulty is in getting one in a nice soft place. Otherwise, you might get a complete rest. Personally, I don't want another anywhere. At present, there is a bombardment on, after which the left flank is going to charge. We are in the centre I'm glad to say and we are not in to-day's show. We expect to charge in a few days. I seem to have been in at everything so far and only hope I come through this next lot as well as I did the last. The Turks have started replying to our shell fire now and they keep getting our trench. I can assure you I'm pretty low down writing this letter. It won't be censored so I can wander on and write to my hearts content. Ernie Shaw, I hear, has been sent down to the Base with Dysentry. Poor beggar looked bad last time I saw him eight days ago. Jack has gone with his sprained ankle and both of them will get a bit of a rest. Let's hope they are away until this next advance is over.

Whilst in the firing line, no less than 14 letters came up for me. I nearly got eyestrain reading them. I got one from you dated sometime in May, one from Mr Price, A. Shaw (financier), Marie Worsley, Billy Lawrence, about 7 from his sister, a lot from Cissie, one from Mr

Adamson, one from Ridley and another from Ma. They had all chased me round from here to Hospital, Convalescent Depot, the Base. and then again on to the Peninsula. It speaks well for the Postal system, doesn't it? I can quite imagine you wanting to have a go with a rifle and ammunition, but the full pack, long marches and fatigues make a soldier's life unbearable. I was doing a bit of sniping yesterday. I fired about 50 rounds at a digging party. They couldn't tell where the shots were coming from and they kept throwing up the job and getting down to it. It was rather good sport. Like you, I could just do with going out with my rifle and ammunition and coming back to a nice dug-out for meals and sleep. This morning I read an article in the Sunday Chronicle of 11/7/15 by Arthur Harrison, on the Dardanelles Mystery. Have you read it? Harrison ought to be interned as a Pro-German for writing such a pessimistic article. I think he'll alter his tune after this week. It's a good job we're not as pessimistic as he. People talk and write articles in the papers and they don't know anything at all of what they're talking or writing about.

At present 160 guns are blazing away as hard as they can and I can't hear myself write. The machine guns are also clacking away and it reminds you of Belle Vue Fireworks on a large scale. We've had some new Officers, brand new ones from Southport where the shrimps come from and they aren't half a green lot. We've also had two draughts sent out - 50 at first and then another 80. The first lot were sent to replace those invalided from Khartoum and the other those we lost in our first bout. I expect the draught to replace the losses of 4th June are on the way out. Somebody was saying that our Division would have been a complete failure had it not been for our Brigade. It's a fact and they don't half give us a working out. Our Brigade comprises Stretford Road lot, the Ardwicks, the Wiganers and our mob and between us I think we could only raise a full Battn. now.

The battleships have now started firing and the noise is awful. We've just had a piece of shell as big as an apple drop between the next chap and me. It brought the top of the parapet off and nearly smothered us. By Jove, I wouldn't like to be a Turk. It must be hellish for the beggars.

Our left has just charged and it was a glorious sight. I've been watching them through a periscope and it was grand. They all wear shining tin plates on their backs so that the Artillery can see them advance and increase the range of the guns. It was a glorious sight but it's risky looking over the top at them so I've got down again and am now writing. It's the good old 29th Division again. By Jove, they have done some charging. They go like a pack of wolves. In the Gallipoli landing they never got mentioned for ages. It was all the Australians and New Zealanders. It was the 29th Division who did the work. The Colonial troops, of course, are great boys but they landed higher up at Gaba Tepe where they were not expected. Of course you will have read Sir Ian Hamilton's report. To see the place they stormed with the bayonet, you'd think it was, indeed, as impregniable as anything on earth. We landed about 8 days afterwards. Had we been at hand a fortnight sooner with a few more Divisions nothing could have stopped us from getting to Constantinople. I suppose this is old news to you as I know you will be studying it pretty hard.

I must chuck it now. I'm really too excited to write so I will conclude. Excuse bad writing and composition, won't you. I'll guess I'd get it hot if the Censor got hold of this letter but I can't see where I've given any information which would be of any use to the enemy, can you? Well, Uncle, I'm still alright and hoping for the best and a speedy downfall for the Turks. Don't worry yourselves, will you? Heaps of love to Marny, Cissie and everybody else. Hope you are all keeping your hearts up. Ta ta. Cheers!

I remain
Your loving nephew
Matt

P.S. For Goodness sake, don't let anybody see this letter or I'll get shot or something dreadful. Write soon.

Letter 47 (postcard) - 16th Aug 1915

No 17 Gen Hosp.
Alexandria
16/8/15

My dear Uncle,

Had left arm amputated at shoulder yesterday. Doing alright.

Matt

Letter 48 - 18th August 1915

Balcony	17 General Hospital
Aug. 18th 1915	Brit. Exped. Force
	Mediterranean

My dear Auntie

Just a few lines to let you know I am wounded and in this hospital. I have had my left arm taken off and am getting on as well as possible. Do not worry as I shall be all right soon. Please write to me at this address. I am trusting in God. With love to all.

I remain your loving nephew

Matt.

Written for me by a red cross helper.   L.S.

Letter 49 - 27th August 1915

17 General Hospital
Brit. Exped. Force
Mediterranean

Balcony Ward 1.

August 27th 1915

My dear Cissie

I am still sticking it and hope to be sent home as soon as I am able to be moved. It will be rather a long job but I am hoping for the best and hope I am able to come carol singing at Christmas. Buck my dear Auntie and Uncle up as much as you can and don't let them worry about me. Give my love to Evelyn. tell her I hope to see her soon. With heaps of love to all at home

I remain yr loving brother
Matt

Written for me by a red cross helper. L.S.

Letter 50 (telegram) - 28th August 1915

ALEXANDRIA STATION.   RUE DU TÉLÉGRAPHE ANGLAIS.

TELEGRAM

THE EASTERN TELEGRAPH
COMPANY LIMITED   REPLIES SHOULD BE ORDERED   *Via Eastern*

Nr Station . .	Clerk's name & date	Time received	No.
DAX 18	J ROSSI 28 AUG 1915	1 – 21	329

MANCHESTER 14 26 TR PASLN = EFM =

POTE RICHARDSON 2263 1/7TH MANCHESTERS 17 GENERAL
HOSPITAL ALEX =

FONDEST LOVE FROM ALL = RICHARDSON   +

Letter 51 - 3rd September 1915

No 17 General Hospital
M. E. F.
Alexandria   3/9/15

My dear Cissie,

I am feeling better today and trying to write you a letter myself. I am laying on my back so 'cuse writing. I was so glad to get the Cablegram. It made me long to be home though! My left wing has been off nearly 3 weeks now but it feels on. It's rotten getting the pain from an arm that isn't there eh? I believe I've only another 5 weeks before the nerves of the old arm die. I had a fearful time on the boat coming over. It was an emergency Transport and I was laying in a Horse box. There was no grub eatable on board. I lived on brandy every 4 hours. It took me 8 days to get to Hospital from being hit and talk about a nightmare! I went under chloroform 3 times on the ship and twice I was too weak so had to be operated on without. I got in this Hospital late at night and they whipped my arm off the next afternoon. Just got it off in time. It's a Septic wound so you can understand it will take ages to get clean out here. Wish I was home. Heaps of love to Marny, my Uncle and everybody.

I remain,
Your loving brother
Matt.   xxxxxxx

Letter 52 - 10th September 1915

Dormitory Block Balcony
17 General Hospital
Alexandria
10/9/15

My dear Uncle,

What ho! I'm up and learning to walk again. I'm about as fat as a match and my knees are of the cab-horse type as yet. Still it's fine to get off one's back as it gets awfully sore. Yesterday I got some letters - one from Cissie and Ma - and a box of cigarettes from Teddy. The excitement might have been the death of me but I survived. I got a very nice letter from Mr Price - more like an illuminated address. He is a sport - he's written me quite a lot of letters but with everything else they're lost. It's marvellous when you're badly wounded how you lose your belongings. I came in Hospital with nothing but trousers and tunic and an old shirt saturated in blood. My coat and trousers were also hard with blood. That was my chief danger - the loss of blood. When they operated they had to inject about two pints of some liquid into me.

My wound isn't quite clean yet and so hasn't started to heal. The invisable arm is still there and still causes me continuous pain. It's awfully strange isn't it feeling pain from an arm that isn't there? I'm glad to hear you and Marny had a good holiday and sorry that I interupted it. I must chuck it now and lie low for a bit. So with heaps of love to Marny, Betty and everybody at home

I remain
Your affectionate nephew
Matt.

P.S. Write soon and don't worry yourselves.

P.P.S. I'm still coming home on the next boat. Don't think it will be long now.

Letter 53 - 12th September 1915

Dormitory Block Balcony,
No 17 General Hospital,
Alexandria, Egypt.
12th September 1915.

Dear Mr Harrison,

I was pleased to receive your letter dated 1st Aug. yesterday and also the letter of congratulations from the Managers. I am also pleased that I am now able to sit up and reply personally to your most welcome letter. Previously I have had to dictate my letters to Red Cross Sisters but this isn't very satisfactory. I am doing fine now and am able to prowl round the ward. It is grand to get on one's feet again after having a month in bed, and now I expect to get well by leaps and bounds. I cannot do much leaping and bounding as yet though! Yesterday I gave myself a much-needed shave and I am fast becoming independent of left arms. My wound isn't clean yet and so hasn't started to heal. Egypt is a bad place for Septic wounds and I think the sooner I get sent to England the sooner it will heal up. The doctors seem satisfied with it's progress, however, and so long as they are, I am. It gets dressed twice every day and I have a very enjoyable ? time on both occasions.

It is very gratifying to know that the Managers and all the Office Staff take such a keen interest in our doings and their appreciation of "our little bit" is very encouraging.

I am glad to hear that Mr Hargreaves is so proud of the Dept.'s record for military service.

In regard to your brother Ted, whilst wishing with all my heart that he is a prisoner of war, I cannot think that it is possible. It was our second night in action and we were going over the open to reinforce the firing line. Star-shells and rockets went up and we were spotted.

Machine-guns and rifle fire scattered us in all directions and I don't think a quarter of us reached the firing line. I was lucky enough to get there but things were about as desperate as they possibly could be. The Turks made four attacks that night and on one occasion got to within 20 yards of our trench. Our ammunition was almost all gone and our Captain told us all to fix our bayonets and prepare to use them. However dawn came and the Turks went back to their trench. A lot of our chaps turned up next day after wandering about all night, others found their way to the Base and the remainder were either killed, wounded or missing. Now, do you think that was a night for taking prisoners? We heard of two or three of our Battalion who are in Constantinople but they were taken prisoners a few weeks afterwards. After the Charge of the 4th June a lot of the 6th Manchesters were left dead on the barbed wire in front of the Turkish trench. They were there when I left last time and although they are dead and can be seen plainly from our trench, they are put down as "missing." It seems they cannot report a man as dead until they identify him. Still we can live in hopes until Turkey is squashed and all her prisoners released. The Turks are far superior, in their methods, to the Germans.

I was sorry to hear of Mr Beaumont's death. By Jove! you must have to stay burning the midnight oil at the Office now. I think you all deserve War medals for sticking at it so well.

I must conclude now. Excuse bad writing. The pen is a beast and I cannot get in a comfortable position. Please give my respects to the Managers, Mr Hargreaves and all in the Dept. I hope I am sent to England soon, Manchester preferred.

With hopes for a speedy end to the War I will finish. There is no doubt as to who is going to win. I think we ought to try to manage without Conscription. What do you think?

> Kind regards,
> I remain,
> Yours sincerely,
> Matt.

Letter 54 (postcard) - 24th September 1915

Friday
24/9/15

Dear Uncle,

Arrived in S'hampton this morning and am now on Hospital Train for the North. Most likely M/c.

We came from Alex on S S Egypt in the record time of 8 days. We had a good passage. Hope you are all in the pink. Will let you know where I get to as soon as I can. So long. Love to all.

Matt

Letter 55 (postcard) - 24th September 1915

A2 Ward
Alfred St Military Hospital
Harpurhey   24/9/15

Dear Kid,

I'm here. Arrived at 7 pm.

Ta ta.

Matt

Letter 56 - 28th September 1915

Alfred St Military Hospital*
Harpurhey M/c
28th Septr 1915

Dear Kid,

I received yr letter this morning. I have got your gloves and hanky alright. I found my way to the Sister's heart this morning and she says that the family can come any day between 2 and 4 but not more than two. So that may facilitate matters for other people to come on Visiting days. Only, kid, if anybody comes, please tell them "No parcels by request." Tell them to save 'em all until I get well and then I'll come round to their houses and collect them. Albert Shaw and Marsh came round last night but they wouldn't let them in. Hard lines, wasn't it? I expect they didn't know how to rush the Guard. Am looking forward to to-morrow and to seeing you again to have that long pow-wow. It's sickening restricting it to two hours, ain't it? I've been doing quite a lot of writing. Am just going to write Mrs Thomas. Ta ta. Don't forget about coming on any day 2 to 4 animals feeding Entrance. Fee 2[d] each. Don't tease the animals or put sticks through the bars.

Au revoir
Matt   xxxxxx

[P.S.] Love to all at home. Looking forward to seeing Marny and my Uncle to-morrow.

*[Matt had at first written 'Alfred St Police Station', indicating the building's peacetime use. The words 'Police Station' were then crossed out and replaced by 'Military Hospital']

Letter 57 - October 1915

Dear Kid,

We've dropped from the frying pan into the fire. We got nothing to eat but drops of milk until after dinner yesterday. Now we're both on FULL Diet. This is breakfast bread and margarine and custard. Lunch bread and marg. Dinner hasn't appeared yet so I don't know what that is. Tea bread and marg. and syrup, and supper bread and marg. and custard. So you see bread and marg. is the staple food here. The only consolation is that Maloney and I are both together in a little room and manage to keep each the other from getting low spirited. The nurses aren't bad but my wound only gets dressed once in the 24 hours whereas it was getting done 6 times down there when I left. It was beginning to look clean but now I suppose it will get yet another set-back. I came here for Erysypilus* but up to now they've done nothing for it. It's better nearly, and I don't know if they are still going to stick to us. I don't think so.

They'll send us back as soon as the infection has gone. I won't be sorry to get back to that little room again even. Well, I don't know about Visitors. Wed and Sat. are the days. You might bring some eggs. I'm feeling O.K. and in the best of spirits. I tell you, I'll take a lot of knocking out. They seem to be doing their utmost here in M/c to crease me but I refuse to turn my toes up.

Well I hope to see somebody on Wed. You get a Pass at the Lodge. The nurse talks about seeing me through the window but I don't know how you'll do it. Well ta ta. Love to Auntie and Uncle.

Matt xxx

*[Erysipelas]

148

Letter 58 (postcard) - October 1915 Monsall Hospital

Dear Kid,

You can come up on Sunday. You can retain the pass for regular and work it in twos.

Matt

Roehampton Hospital 1916. Matt is third from the right in the third row down.

Letter 59 - 13th July 1916
Letter from Matt's Commanding Officer

7th Battn. Manchester Regt.

Headquarters

Burlington Street

Manchester

13. 7. 1916

Dear Richardson.

Please accept the enclosed from me as a memento of a great day in your life, the particulars of all the others that received the DCM at the same time. Should be of interest to you and yours for many years.

All good wishes

Yours truly

H G Davies

Major

[Enclosed with this letter was a typed list of other medal recipients, with a short paragraph about each man. This list has also survived]

Matt's later life

Matt's postcard (to his sister Cissie) from Monsall Hospital (an isolation hospital in north Manchester which has since been closed and demolished) was the last he wrote in this collection of letters. Together with the two letters to John Harrison at Refuge Assurance, the draft of John Harrison's reply to one of them and the final letter from Matt's commanding officer, all the letters that have survived are those Matt sent to his immediate family at 91 Cromwell Road, Stretford and kept by them (probably by his sister Cissie, as only three of Matt's letters to his great aunt Jane have survived) as a memento of the extraordinary year he spent away from them serving in the Middle East. Matt wrote many other letters during that year to other members of his family, friends and colleagues at Refuge Assurance, but these have not survived as far as is known. Matt may well have continued to write to them after this date, as his separation from them was not yet over. Shortly after sending the last postcard, Matt suffered a serious relapse in his condition, possibly as a result of poor treatment at Monsall Hospital. He required many months of further nursing and then rehabilitation before he was able to pull through. For this, he was sent to Roehampton Military Hospital in London. Roehampton House was requisitioned in 1915 by the War Office for limbless ex-servicemen. The hospital still has an amputee unit. Eventually, Matt was considered fit enough to be discharged as 'medically unfit for further service' eleven months later, on 13th September 1916. On 5th June 1916, Matt attended the ceremony at Manchester town hall at which he was presented with his Distinguished Conduct Medal, by Lt General Sir Pitcairn Campbell.

Matt's delayed return to civilian life, due to his injuries, did not prevent considerable local media interest in the first local man to be awarded such a medal. Matt's collection of newspaper and magazine cuttings also included a special recruiting poster and a golden illuminated certificate of appreciation from the Stretford Urban District Council.

Judging from the collection of memorabilia, photographs and letters that he kept, it seems that he may have intended to make a record of his experiences during the year he spent on active service. The completion of a correspondence course in journalism later is possibly another indication of this intention.

Following his rehabilitation at Roehampton and his final discharge from the army, Matt returned home to resume life with his beloved Aunt Jane, Uncle Nicholas and big sister Cissie, at 91 Cromwell Road. The loss of an arm must have meant radical adjustments to his social activities. Before the war, Matt had been a keen sportsman, a member of Stretford AFC and Refuge AFC football clubs, a member of the Refuge water polo team and an excellent tennis player. Coming to terms with his disability must have been particularly hard in relation to his sporting activities, but Matt's undaunted spirit is evidenced by the fact that he and his younger brother Rid became formidable players on the local tennis circuit as a three-handed doubles team as well as singles players.

Uncle Nicholas died in 1926 at the age of 78.

When Matt joined the army, his sister Cissie had already met her husband to be, Harold Adamson, and they eventually married after a long courtship. Matt's reluctance to leave his ageing aunt eventually caused the break-up of his long-standing engagement to a friend of his brother's future wife. She could not face the prospect of sharing her married life with Aunt Jane. Another friend from Matt's pre-army days, Evelyne Lawrence, helped him to overcome the deep emotional upset he found difficult to deal with. It proved to be a true love match and they were married in July 1928. Matt said that Evelyne was the only girl he had been able to put both arms around. Evelyne's philosophical approach to life was a great asset when she and Matt found out later that they could not have children.

Aunt Jane died in 1936 at the age of 85.

Evelyne was a talented amateur actress and photographs survive of the many stage productions she took part in over the years. Matt and Evelyne were well known throughout their life together for their abilities to entertain at parties, clubs, holiday outings and social gatherings at their church. Matt was renowned for his jokes and monologues, Evelyne for her singing. Both were members of the Hallé Choir for many years.

Following his discharge from the army, Matt returned to his post in the legal department at the Refuge Assurance Company. He rapidly learned to cope with only one arm. A small souvenir defused cannon shell became a partial substitute for his missing arm, being used as a paperweight on his desk in the office and in later life at home. He stayed with the Refuge for the rest of his working life, reaching management rank before he retired at the age of sixty. His younger brother Ridley, who joined the legal department at Refuge Assurance as a clerk not long after Matt's period of war service, also later achieved management rank with the company before his retirement.

Matt, who never wanted to go overseas again, died after a short illness on 18 September 1964, at the age of seventy-one. Evelyne survived him by almost thirty-one years, but was able to look back on a long and very happy marriage.

Notes

Extract from the Richardson and Ridley family history

Matt's father, who was also called Matthew Ridley Richardson, was only two years old when both his parents, Thomas and Sarah (née Ridley), died of typhoid fever in their early twenties. He was brought up by his grandfather, Jimmy Richardson, and from the age of 16, by his mother's brother Nicholas and her sister Jane, both unmarried. He became a journeyman-joiner and married Maria Newton from Liverpool. His work often took him away from home and these absences gradually became longer and longer, eventually extending to years at a time, leaving his ever growing family without any support from him. His occasional visits home could result in the birth of yet another child, adding to the burden Maria had to cope with on her own.

Matthew junior and his sister Cissie were adopted by their great uncle Nicholas and great aunt Jane to ease the burden. Nicholas and Jane had moved to 91 Cromwell Road, Stretford, in the early 1890s. It was known as the 'ancestral home' by the family.

Matt's sister Cissie (Sarah Elizabeth) married Harold Adamson, who is also mentioned in Matt's letters. Cissie and Harold remained in the Manchester area for the rest of their lives, although Cissie survived her husband by many years. She died in April 1975 at the age of 88. As is indicated in Matt's letters, one of Cissie's great interests was music and she was a talented pianist.

Matt's elder brother Ted (Teddy) is mentioned frequently in Matt's letters. Matt felt a particular kinship with his brother Ted, who had also joined the army, but was serving on the Western Front with the Royal Engineers. Although Ted survived the war, married, and lived into old age, he was deeply scarred by what was then called shellshock which blighted the rest of his life.

Medals

Matt received four medals in consequence of his war service:

Distinguished Conduct Medal

Instituted during the Crimean War in 1854, the Distinguished Conduct Medal was a military decoration of the second rank, awarded to non-commissioned officers and other ranks of the British army for "individual acts of distinguished conduct in the field." It was equivalent to the Distinguished Service Order for commissioned officers, although below it in precedence. It was usually seen as a 'near miss' for the Victoria Cross. It was replaced, along with the DSO, by the Conspicuous Gallantry Cross, awarded to all ranks, from 1993.

1914-1915 Star

Awarded to officers and men of British and Imperial forces who served in any theatre of war between 5th August 1914 and 31st December 1915. The medal was approved in 1918.

British War Medal 1914-1918

Awarded to officers and men of British and Imperial forces who had rendered service between 5th August 1914 and 11th November 1918. The medal was approved in 1919.

Victory Medal - United Kingdom (Allied Victory Medal) 1914-1919

This was awarded to those who had received the 1914 Star or the 1914-1915 Star, and the British War Medal. It was an international award - other states that were at war with Germany, Austria and Turkey issued their own versions of this medal.

The Third Battle of Krithia

The Second Battle of Krithia, in early May 1915, had had as its objectives a general advance from the beachheads on the tip of the peninsula and the capture of the village of Krithia and the hill of Achi Baba. From Achi Baba, the Turks had a commanding view over all the Allied positions on the tip of the peninsula and could subject the entire Allied-held territory to constant shellfire. If the Allies were able to capture Achi Baba, they would hold a similar advantage over Turkish forces north and east of the hill, facilitating an Allied advance further up the peninsula. In the Second Battle of Krithia, the Allies failed to attain these objectives, their advance being only a few hundred yards at a cost of more than 6000 casualties in the face of strong Turkish opposition.

The British commander at Gallipoli, General Aylmer Hunter-Weston, advised the War Office that greater forces would be needed if another attempt were to have any chance of success. By late May, British reinforcements had arrived in Gallipoli, including elements of 42 Division from Egypt and the Sudan. This was deemed sufficient for a further attempt.

In the event, the objectives for the Third Battle were limited to a general advance of the front line towards Krithia with the capture of the village being the most that might be expected. Prior to the battle, between the 27th and 29th May, the British managed to advance their front line by stealth, a distance of about 200 yards, so that the front was within charging distance of the Turkish line. This was achieved by men crawling out into no-man's land at night to establish a new front line. Each man carried two sandbags and a shovel. Using the sandbags to shelter behind, each man dug a hole five paces from that of the next man. When the holes were deep enough to stand up in, the men would then dig through to link them so as to form a continuous trench. Men of the 7th Battalion of the Manchester Regiment were out in no-man's land on the night of 28th May. As well as being hard work, it was also dangerous, with Turkish snipers taking a toll of casualties - as Matthew Richardson described in his letter of 2nd June.

By early June, the Allies had positioned their forces. The French held the front from the Dardanelles shore to the Kereves Spur. To their left, the Royal Naval Division held the front from the north flank of Kereves Spur to Krithia Nullah, a dry watercourse. To their left again, the 42nd Division (including the units of the Manchester Regiment) held the front from Krithia Nullah to Fir Tree Spur. In detail, the battalions of the Manchester Regiment held the line from Krithia Nullah to the ground to the north of the road or track that led to Krithia village along the north side of Krithia Nullah. The 6th Battalion held the left wing of the Manchesters' section of the line. The 8th Battalion held position astride the road to Krithia. The 5th Battalion was to their right, and the 7th Battalion held the right wing in positions astride the Krithia Nullah watercourse. Their line of advance was along the dried watercourse where trees and bushes would give them cover but would also give cover to Turkish gun and sniper positions. To the left of the 42nd Division, the 29th Division held the front from Fir Tree Spur to the Aegean shore, supported by the 29th Indian Brigade and the Lancashire Fusiliers from Gully Ravine and over Gully Spur to the Aegean shore.

The attack began on 4th June, and was preceded by the usual artillery bombardment. This was much weaker than for a comparable operation on the Western Front. At the Third Battle of Krithia, the British only had 78 guns and howitzers. Although there was also supporting gunfire from naval vessels, these were firing whilst under way in order to reduce the risks from torpedo attack and so their accuracy was much reduced. There was a 'false end' to the bombardment to draw the Turks out of their shelters to man their front line. The bombardment of the Turkish line then resumed, causing heavy Turkish casualties. But because of the shortage of guns, the bombardment had been insufficient to destroy key Turkish strongholds and this affected the outcome of the battle.

The advance began at noon. The French immediately ran up against Turkish strongholds in Kereves Dere (another dry watercourse) and on Kereves Spur that had escaped the bombardment and they were unable to make any progress. To their left, the Royal Naval Division had greater success. Led by the 2nd Naval Brigade and using armoured cars to advance along Krithia Spur they reached and captured the Turkish trenches. However, when the second wave, who were intended to 'leapfrog' the first wave, attempted to continue the advance, they were caught in enfilade fire from Turkish strongholds on Kereves Spur which it had been expected would have been in French hands by then. The second wave (the Collingwood Battalion) suffered very heavy casualties and although they managed to achieve a further advance, the fire from the Turkish strongholds on Kereves Spur made their position untenable. Before the end of the day, they had had to withdraw to their start positions.

The 42nd Division had the greatest success of the day. Led by the Manchester Brigade (made up of units of the Manchester Regiment), they quickly reached their first objective of capturing the Turkish front line trenches and then advanced well beyond, breaking through the Turkish 9th Division, to a total distance of about 1000 yards and capturing more than 200 prisoners. A and C Companies of the 7th Battalion of the Manchesters advanced along Krithia Nullah and took the Turkish front line trench. B and D Companies then pushed on for another 500 yards or more, taking the second line of the Turkish trenches. They came under enfilade fire from their right from trenches still in Turkish hands, but they managed to hold the ground they had taken. The Manchester Battalions took a heavy toll of casualties in this advance. In his letter of 9th June, Matthew Richardson wrote that his battalion was down to only 120 men and 3 officers (i.e. not killed or wounded). Only 160 men of the 6th Battalion had escaped death or injury with one company being reduced to 18 men. (A company was about 200 men and a battalion about 800 men). Major J H Staveacre, commander of Matthew Richardson's company, was killed early on in the attack, as was Lt Col W G Heys who had taken command of the Manchester Brigade when Brig Gen Noel Lee, commander of the Manchester Brigade, was mortally wounded. Arrangements for getting the seriously wounded (stretcher cases) back to the Advance Dressing Station, and thence to the beachhead for evacuation, were inadequate and often chaotic with many stretcher bearers becoming casualties themselves.

On the left wing of the front, the attack was less successful. Apart from an advance by the Gurkha Rifles along the shoreline, the Indian Brigade was able to make little progress with a battalion of the Ferozepore Sikh Regiment being almost wiped out in Gully Ravine. The left of the 29th Division's advance along Fir Tree Spur was thus exposed to Turkish fire. Elsewhere the advance of the 29th Division was halted with heavy casualties inflicted by Turkish strongholds that had survived the initial artillery bombardment.

With the attack failing on the two flanks, General Hunter-Weston attempted to bolster the flanks by sending reinforcements there instead of to the centre where the attack had been successful. But the 29th Division, pinned down by Turkish fire, was unable to make any further progress and, on the right of the line, the French also insisted that they were unable to advance. At 1600 hrs, Hunter-Weston ordered the troops along the line to dig in where they were. At this point, the Turks launched a counter-attack. The Manchester Brigade, now in an exposed salient, was attacked on three sides. It was decided that the position in the salient was untenable and the Manchesters were ordered to withdraw to their first objective, the original Turkish front line. The following day, the Turks launched a further counter-attack to try and recover their front line. It was at this moment that Matthew Richardson fought the action that earned him the DCM, single-handedly repelling repeated attempts by the Turks to retake a trench which then formed part of the British front line. By the end of the battle, the new front line was only some 200 to 250 yards in front of the start line, passing through an area known as The Vineyard in the centre, which was to see further fighting in August.

As a result of the battle, the Allies suffered some 6500 casualties, killed and injured. One of the injured was Matthew Richardson, who had been struck a glancing blow by a bullet above his left eye. He was evacuated to Cairo where he made a full recovery and by mid-July he was back in the trenches in Gallipoli.

The Battle of Krithia Vineyard

In order to try to break the stalemate at Gallipoli that had existed since the initial landings in April 1915, a new landing was planned for early August at Suvla Bay, just north of Anzac Cove, one of the original beachheads. It was hoped that this would enable the Allied forces to achieve the breakout from the beachheads that had so far eluded them. The landing was to take place on 6th August and, in order to draw Turkish forces away from Suvla Bay, diversionary offensives were launched on both the Cape Helles and Anzac Cove fronts.

At Cape Helles, the attack was made in the centre of the line by the 88th Brigade of the 29th Division and the 126th and 127th Brigades of the 42nd Division. The 29th Division attacked first on 6th August. As on previous occasions, there was a shortage of guns and so the supporting artillery was not strong enough to be effective (although there was also gunfire from naval vessels as Matthew Richardson recorded in his letter of 6th August). Twice during the course of that day, the 88th Brigade reached and captured the Turkish trenches in the front line opposite, but each time the Turks counter-attacked and drove them back, inflicting heavy casualties. By the end of the day, the 88th Brigade was back at the start line with nothing to show for all the men they had lost.

The following day, the 42nd Division launched an attack from positions immediately to the right of the 29th Division. The 127th Brigade, which included the 1/7th Manchesters, managed to break through the Turkish front line, only to be driven back by another Turkish counter-attack. During the next two days, the Turks counter-attacked several times as the men of the 42nd grimly hung on to the small advance they had managed to make in a former vineyard which was to give the battle its name. Following the Turkish counter-attacks, the fighting had largely died down by 13th August as Turkish attention focused on the action at Suvla Bay. For what was supposed to be only a diversionary attack, the British suffered nearly 4,000 casualties, killed and injured, for a minimal change in the front line. As a diversion it also failed, as the Turks prevented an Allied breakout at Suvla Bay and kept the Allied forces blockaded on the beachhead there. It was the beginning of the end of the ill-fated Gallipoli campaign.

Among the casualties was Matthew Richardson, whose left arm was mangled by bullets or shrapnel. He was one of the lucky ones. He was recovered to the British lines and eventually put on a hospital ship bound for Alexandria. His account of the nightmare voyage is given in Letter 51, dated 3rd September 1915. On arrival in hospital in Alexandria, his left arm was amputated at the shoulder, as it was too badly damaged to be saved. For a while Matt's life hung in the balance before he began a long, slow recovery that continued after he was evacuated back to England in late September. It was to be another month after that before the British accepted that the intervention in Gallipoli was a failure and began planning an evacuation of the peninsula.

The Manchester Regiment

The Manchester Regiment was created in 1881 from an amalgamation of the 63rd and the 96th Regiments of Foot and two battalions of the Royal Lancashire Militia. The 63rd and 96th Regiments had been widely involved in campaigns associated with the establishment of the British Empire during the eighteenth and nineteenth centuries. There had also been involvement in the Crimean War and, following the formation of the regiment, the Boer War.

After the outbreak of the First World War, new battalions of the regiment were raised as the Army expanded in 1914 and 1915. At the start of the war, the regiment had had two active battalions of the Regular Army formed of professional or career soldiers. From August 1914, new battalions were raised as part of the Territorial Force. The 1/5th to the 1/10th Battalions were the first set to be raised on 4th August 1914, followed by the 2/5th to 2/10th and the 3/5th to 3/10th. Additionally, nine 'Pals' Battalions' from the Manchester area were attached to the regiment, forming its 16th to 24th Battalions. Three further battalions were formed of men who had responded to Lord Kitchener's appeal for volunteers ('Kitchener's Army'), becoming the 11th to 13th Battalions. During the course of the war, ten garrison, reserve and training battalions were also attached to the regiment.

Battalions of the Manchester Regiment were involved in almost all the major campaigns of the British army during the First World War. This included involvement in most of the major battles on the Western Front from 1914 to 1918. Elsewhere, they took part in the campaigns in Egypt and Palestine, Gallipoli, Macedonia, Italy and Mesopotamia.

The 1/7th Battalion remained in Gallipoli until the final evacuation of Allied forces and, in January 1916, they were moved to Egypt. In June 1916 they were stationed at Kantara as part of the forces defending the Suez Canal. They were involved in actions defending the canal and in the early stages of the advance towards Palestine. In March 1917, the battalion was recalled to Europe for service on the Western Front where they arrived in April. Initially stationed on the Somme front opposite the Hindenburg Line, in August they were moved to the Flanders front. In March 1918 the battalion was back on the Somme front, heavily involved in the fighting that eventually managed to stop the German spring offensive of that year. Following the failure of the German advance, the 1/7th was involved in the Allied counter attack that brought about the final collapse of German forces and the end of the war. The 11th November 1918 found the battalion in positions around the town of Maubeuge.

In the Second World War, battalions of the Manchester Regiment formed part of the British Expeditionary Force and were involved in the evacuation of the BEF from Dunkirk. In 1944, battalions of the Manchesters were part of the breakout from the Normandy beachheads and the advance across northern France, the Low Countries and into north-west Germany. Elsewhere, the Manchesters were involved in the campaigns in the Mediterranean and Italy and in the Far East. The latter included the fall of Singapore, the battle of Kohima (which ended Japanese attempts to invade India) and the Burma campaign.

Postwar, the Manchester Regiment formed part of the British Army of the Rhine. In 1958 the regiment was amalgamated with the King's Regiment (Liverpool) to form the King's Regiment (Manchester and Liverpool).

The main depot of the Manchester Regiment was in Ashton-under-Lyne. However, the 1/7th Battalion was attached to the depot in Burlington Street, Manchester.

The Lee-Enfield Rifle

While he was a soldier, Matthew Richardson's constant companion was his rifle. It would have been his responsibility to clean it and maintain it in working order. Although the standard infantry weapon of the British army by 1914 was the Short Magazine Lee-Enfield Mark III rifle, the battalions of the Manchester Regiment in Egypt and Sudan, and subsequently Gallipoli, were equipped with the earlier long-barrelled Lee-Enfield rifle (Magazine Lee-Enfield Mk I* - the use of a magazine was still a relatively recent development, hence its acknowledgement in the name of the weapon). This was a bolt-action rifle with a magazine of ten rounds which were loaded in two clips of five rounds. A spring in the magazine fed the bullets upwards and, the bolt being open or pulled back, one cartridge was pressed out of the magazine. Sliding the bolt forward pushed the cartridge into the chamber and cocked the rifle. Once fired, pulling the bolt back again ejected the spent cartridge case and the firing sequence started again. A trained soldier was able to fire at least twenty rounds a minute. The extreme range of the weapon was about 3,700 yards, although effective range was 500 to 600 yards. The rifle weighed 9lb 8 ounces; it was 4ft 1½ins long with a barrel length of 30.2 inches. It fired a .303 inch calibre bullet with a muzzle velocity of about 2000 feet per second. Also standard equipment was a long sword bayonet which was attached to the rifle by a spring catch. The firing mechanism and most of the barrel were encased in a wooden body or frame (the 'fore-end' of the stock), which formed the forward grip for the left hand. The butt or shoulder rest was also of wood.

The long-barrelled Lee-Enfield was adopted by the British army in 1895. The Short (barrelled) Magazine Lee-Enfield (SMLE) Mk I was introduced in 1904, and the SMLE Mk III, a modified version, was introduced in 1907. The Lee-Enfield was one of the first rifles adapted to fire cartridges using smokeless powder instead of gunpowder. The name Lee-Enfield derived from James Paris Lee, who invented the bolt mechanism used in the rifle, and the Royal Small Arms Factory at

Enfield, Middlesex, where the rifles were initially manufactured. They were subsequently widely manufactured elsewhere due to wartime demand.

Troopships

S.S. Grandtully Castle - the troopship that took Matt from Southampton to Port Sudan in September 1914.

The S.S. Grandtully Castle, 7,612 tons, was built for the Union Castle Mail Steamship Company in 1910. Commandeered as a troopship at the start of the First World War, she subsequently served as a hospital ship in the eastern Mediterranean (to judge from a surviving photograph). The ship survived the war, returning to service as a passenger ship with Union Castle. Following withdrawal from service, the Grandtully Castle was scrapped in 1939.

S.S. Suevic - the ship that took Matt from Port Sudan to Egypt, en route to the Dardanelles, April 1915.

The 12,531 ton Suevic had a chequered history. Built by Harland and Wolff in 1901 for the White Star Line, she ran hard aground in 1907 on Stag Rock near the Lizard. The bow was separated, and she travelled, under her own steam, to Southampton, where a new bow, made by Harland and Wolff, was fitted. Requisitioned on the outbreak of war in 1914, she was used to transport the Australian cavalry (part of the ANZAC force) from Australia to the Mediterranean. This included their horses - as Matt noted in Letter 25 written on board Suevic which was taking him from Port Sudan to Egypt on his way to the Dardanelles. The ship survived the war and after being withdrawn from service as a liner, she was bought by a Norwegian company in 1940 for use as a whale processing vessel and re-named Skytteren. After the German occupation of Norway, she was interned in Sweden with 15 other ships. During an abortive mass attempt to escape in 1942, the ship was scuttled by her crew before she could be boarded by the waiting Germans who had been notified by the Swedes.

S.S. Ionian - the ship that took Matt and the 1/7th Manchesters from Egypt to Gallipoli in May 1915.

The Ionian was built in Belfast by Workman, Clark & Co. Ltd. for the Allan Line of Liverpool. Launched 12 September 1901, she was 470 feet long and 8,268 tons gross weight. Powered by triple expansion steam engines, she had twin screws, one funnel amidships, four masts, three decks and was fitted with refrigerating machinery. She had accommodation for 131 First Class, 160 Second Class, and 800 Steerage passengers. She was used on north Atlantic routes from Liverpool or Glasgow to Quebec, Montreal, Halifax and Boston. In 1914 she was taken over by the British Government and used as a troopship. In 1917 she was taken over by the Canadian Pacific Line, but in October that year she struck a mine and sank off Milford Haven.

S.S. Southland - the hospital ship that took Matt from Gallipoli to Alexandria in June 1915.

Originally named the SS Vaderland and built by John Brown & Co, Glasgow, for the Red Star Line, a joint US-Belgian shipping company. Launched 12 July 1900, 11899 tons gross, 560.8ft long, two funnels, four masts, twin screw with two quadruple expansion steam engines, 342 First Class, 194 Second Class and 626 Steerage passengers. She was used on the North Atlantic routes, mainly between Antwerp and New York. In 1915 she was requisitioned as a troopship and renamed the Southland (to avoid confusion between the Flemish 'Vaderland' and the German 'Vaterland'). In September 1915, she was torpedoed in the Aegean by the German submarine UB-14 with the loss of 40 lives, but was beached on Lemnos, salvaged and returned to service. However, she was torpedoed again and sunk by the U-70 off the north-west coast of Ireland on 4 June 1917 with the loss of four lives.

S.S.Egypt - the hospital ship in which Matt returned to England in September 1915.

Built by Caird & Co Ltd, Greenock for the P&O Steam Navigation Co, the Egypt was 500ft long, 8000 tons, with twin funnels and single screw. Her maiden voyage in 1897 was to Bombay. She was taken over by the British Government for use as a hospital ship in August 1915 and, the following month, Matt was ferried home in her along with other wounded from the Gallipoli front. The Egypt was used as a hospital ship until 1919, when she was returned to civilian use as a passenger liner.

In 1922 the Egypt was struck amidships in thick fog by a French ship, the Seine, off the coast of Brittany in the Bay of Biscay and sank within 20 minutes with the loss of 86 of her 342 passengers and crew. She was en route to Bombay with a cargo that included £1 million of gold and silver bullion which was not salvaged until the early 1930s.

Matt's mother Maria with Matt's younger brother Harold, about 1912.

Matt's Distinguished Conduct Medal.

A recruitment poster for the Manchester Regiment, citing Matt's DCM.

A photo taken at the medal presentation ceremony outside Manchester Town Hall on 5th June 1916. Matt is in the centre of the picture. To his right is Major General Sir Pitcairn Campbell, who presented the medals. Photo by J Cleworth.

Ted Harrison, brother of John Harrison, Matt's boss at Refuge Assurance. Ted Harrison was killed at Gallipoli.

Matt (kneeling, left) with Stretford AFC, 1911.

Matt's brother Ernest, sister Cissie and her fiancé Harold.

Matt's brother Edward (Ted) Richardson, Royal Engineers 1914-1918.

A dinner party sometime in the 1950s. Lower and middle right, Matt and Evelyne; top left, Matt's brother Ridley (Rid).

Matt and Evelyne in later life.

Matt and his wife Evelyne.

Longford Park (Stretford) Veterans 1962. Matt is the furthest right of those kneeling.

Matt.

Acknowledgements

For general and background information about Egypt, The Sudan and the Gallipoli campaign, and also for the annexes about the Manchester Regiment and the Lee-Enfield rifle, Wikipedia has been an invaluable source.

For details about the battalions of the Manchester Regiment in the Third Battle of Krithia, a website called "More Than A Name - The stories of the men from the Stockport area who fought and died in the Great War 1914-1918" run by John Hartley proved both useful and interesting.

That amazing tool Google Maps, as well as giving views of the battlefields, also gave clues as to the locations of one or two of the unidentified photographs in Matthew Richardson's collection. The views of the battlefields on the Gallipoli peninsula also show how much the whole area is regarded by Turkey as a sombre memorial to its own war dead with monuments rivalling the Menin Gate and other memorials on the Western Front. The Turks lost at least as many men as the Allies during the Gallipoli campaign.